To Eric
with my best
wishes

Letters from England

A perfect journey at the perfect time

by
Patricia Jacobs

Patty Jacobs

Copyright © 2004

Patricia Jacobs

ISBN 0-9763016-0-1

Printed in the U.S.A. by
Morris Publishing
3212 East Highway 30
Kearney, NE 68847
1-800-650-7888

ACKNOWLEDGMENTS

The author wishes to thank Cecelia Hagen, the Meadowlark Memoir Class, and Cynthia Hale for their invaluable help. Cecelia's insightful editing and guidance and Cynthia's technical knowledge has made publication of this book possible.

Front cover: Cambridge University Backs to the Cam River

Back Cover: The back side of Ivy House

for Wes, Doug, David and Tom

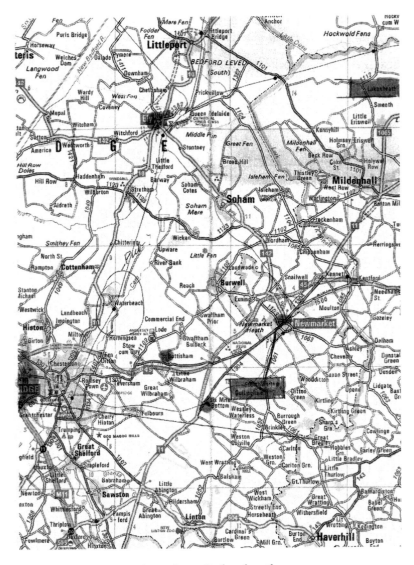

Area from Lakenheath
to Stetchworth

TABLE OF CONTENTS

"Memory is a complicated thing, a relative to truth, but not it's twin."

--Barbara Kingsolver

LETTERS FROM ENGLAND

I ~A DREAM ~

I'm a person who needs to look back— a postcard collector, letter writer, picture-taker. Just days before the trip to my aunt's memorial service, I'd been reading the letters I wrote to my parents during our three year stay in England. Somehow it didn't seem that long ago, remembering a sun-streaked April morning in 1975, when my husband, our three sons and I landed at RAF Mildenhall. At about 2000 feet, under puffy Constable clouds, I could make out the spring-green fields and hedgerows lining the twisty lanes. There was a tiny car and what looked like a dozen sheep straddling a small road—a tractor stopped dead center behind them.

Five hundred feet lower, I had another vision—a rectangular Norman keep at the edge of the village about three city blocks long, the High Street leading to the churchyard and manor house beyond. The picture seemed to step out of a childhood fairytale book.

I'd had a heavy, hard-to-shake dream. I was running down the wooded path toward Devil's Dike. Two short men in coats and ties (fox or pheasant beaters) were closing in. The hunt's not far behind! A barricaded trail ahead. I dodge wet, slippery horse chestnuts, yelling I'm here. Stop. Help! My now grown sons are there, little kids under a huge chestnut collecting nuts like gold nuggets in plastic Marks and Spencer's bags. I yell again, Here! Listen! Please!

A man's emphatic voice announced, "Flight attendants prepare for landing." The bell was sounding, the seatbelt sign lit-up. A soft scratchy Help! escaped my throat. I touched the empty seat beside me. Of course my mother wasn't there, but she had been—at least it seemed so the entire past weekend at Aunt Kathryn's Memorial service.

Looking out the window, I half expected to see Mildenhall Village, the tower of St. Mary's, horses on the heath, or cows grazing near the lazy Cam River. But no, it was February 22, 2004, not April, 1975. Outside it was high noon and sunny. What I saw was Fern Ridge Lake, drained and swampy, a few Sunday drivers in miniature, and the flat, wet farmland surrounding Eugene's airport runway.

Before my aunt's service there had been an intense gathering of family inside the small chapel. Streaks of winter sun filtered through stained glass windows, touching one, then another—familial traits evident on half the faces. Saddened, wide-brown eyes lined with dark lashes and brows, full lips, some dimpled chins. The pictures in the church foyer might have been taken in England. Mother was about twenty-one, Aunt Kathryn five years younger. Both were in jodhpurs and velvet riding hats— their heavy brown side-braids pulled back and knotted into buns below their caps.

Mother had drifted in and out of my dream. I was back in Suffolk, where gardeners, coal merchants, and milkmen wore coats and ties to work, where the lane leading to our village was lined with a canopy of copper beech and chestnut, where riders on hacks wore proper boots and velvet-billed hats, where the boys picked up nuts they called bonkers on Guy Fawke's Day, where one early December my friend Mary Beth and I collected Christmas greens on the Duke's private side of the Devil's Dike trail and came close to being stampeded (or so we thought). We heard a bugle (ta-tet-ta-ta), fell to the ground on top the confiscated greens, and laughed ourselves silly at the headlines we imagined in the Newmarket News—*American Women Caught Stealing From Duke's Estate.*

Dear Mother and Dad,   *June 2nd, 1975*

We're finally moving out of Base Housing—Yeah! Actually it wasn't bad at all if you consider I used those weeks to get the boys settled in their schools, and for all of us to collect our bearings. The best thing may have happened. Wes was in the Officer's Club this noon when a pilot transferring to Germany tacked a rental notice on the board. He called the number immediately, and we have an appointment tomorrow to check it out. I'll let you know if Ivy House Farm is as charming as it sounds...

My husband Wes was ready for a change after 18 years of training and practicing medicine in Oregon. The military needed physicians in the early seventies, and offered enticing incentives— rank, pay, and the prospect of living abroad. Wow! The only war the Cold War with Russians as bad guys—somehow didn't seem much of a threat. Maybe Wes had reached a 'mid-life crisis.' Whatever, after a year of deliberation we decided to make the move to England. It was the onset of some of the most eventful and fun years in our family's life together. Fortunately we couldn't see three years into the future —a future that would bring the ending of this charmed period in our young lives.

The first six weeks weren't that easy for Doug, 17, David, 15, and Tom, 10—changing schools and starting over in a new country at the beginning of spring term when "all the kids had known each other for years." Wes had to deal with the rigors of a new job. My task of finding a place to live was simpler. The hardest part was learning to drive on the wrong side of the road, immediately! The fact that we found a used Morris Minor with a right-hand drive helped. Tom was still small enough so we could squeeze three bodies in the backseat if necessary, but not without a fuss.

"Left Mom! Keep left," the kids yelled for the better part of that first month and more than occasionally thereafter.

We lived temporarily in furnished, dusty-beige (inside and out) base housing with apartment walls so thin you could watch TV with the sound turned off and catch every single word from next door, among other things. After six weeks of house hunting from Ely to Cambridge, and Thetford to Bury St. Edmunds, we lucked out!

Ivy House, with its reed-thatched roof, dated from the 16th century. The village of Stetchworth was three miles from Newmarket and 11 miles from Cambridge—the university of Samuel Pepys, Oliver Cromwell, and Prince Charles, no less—and 60 miles from London. It was as if we'd gotten our own Shangri-La.

RAF Lakenheath was an easy 18-mile drive from Stetchworth. On occasion I'd stop to see the sun set in hues of gold to burnt-orange, to the soft pink of summer and then fade gently into the silent heath. I often detoured on the drive to and from the base through the farmlands and famous stud farms surrounding Newmarket. It wasn't uncommon on the A11 just north of town to have to stop in the early morning and wait while a dozen racehorses, their trainer, and riders crossed the road, the horses shying, steam wisps curling from their nostrils. By summer the small lanes between Stetchworth and the adjoining village of Dullingham were alive with bunnies—visions of "Watership Down," a book we'd read before our move.

Mrs. Cameron, the rental go-between and local newsmonger, had opened the gate and was waiting for us. Her hair was knotted up in a gingham kerchief, minus a few straggly bangs in front. She could have been the woman in a Maytag add, albeit a smidge older, except for her thinly plucked and penciled eyebrows. Wes's wild bear sense of smell detected she'd had fish and chips for lunch.

According to Mrs. Cameron, it had taken four blokes ("what you Americans call hippies") four years and plenty of sweet smelling cigarettes to complete the restoration of Ivy House. To our good fortune the owner, who'd recently moved to Venice, California, decided to take the property off the market, waiting out the economic downturn. Renting to Americans was a safer prospect than leasing to locals who might become squatters with legal rights.

The five of us fell in love with Ivy House Farm before we stepped inside. The grounds were about an acre and partially enclosed with a brick and flint wall—some of it 16th century. A very old birch feathered and shaded the wall from the warm sun. I put my hand on the flint stone that first day, thinking way back in time, wondering how many hands had done the same, how many sons like mine had sat on the wall's smoothed edge.

We drove into a large graveled yard surrounded by outbuildings, a pond, and a cobbled path to the house and climbed out of the Morris. I'm sure I heard four other whew's and light whistles. If Mary Poppins and her outspread umbrella had floated from the roof, it wouldn't have surprised me.

Mrs. Cameron must have been a psychic, suggesting we take a peek in the outbuildings first. The two garages backing onto the High Street held the landlord, Brian's, partially restored '46 Bentley and a 1920s Rolls Royce. Wes, a car enthusiast, could have passed out then and there. She said the buildings were to remain padlocked but assured us Brian wouldn't mind good renters keeping an eye on things—look don't touch.

The dark brown barn (a former slaughter house of historical importance, according to Mrs. Cameron) was literally covered with a magnificent, thick white climbing rose. I was becoming more convinced of her psychic facilities—maybe she'd had a course on how to impress Americans 101—when she looked at me, raised her outlined eyebrows and said, "It's a dusty mess in here, but you'll love it, dearie."

Brian was also an aspiring antique dealer. Half the barn was piled high with old furniture and lots of it junk. On closer inspection I noticed a number of Victorian objects, some horse and rider statuary (Greek and Roman copies I'm sure), jardinières of various sizes and shapes, a few twenties-Art Nouveau lamps and ashtrays, pitchers and basins, and at least one night bucket.

"Should you sign on, this stuff's for sale," she said, taking a deep breath and wiping her brown-spotted hands on her freshly starched apron, as if to say she wasn't in the least interested. "The good things are inside."

7

Next to the barn was a small paddock and two loose boxes (miniscule unless the horses were Shetland ponies), that could be leased for a peppercorn rent from the Duke of Sutherland's estate. There was also a good-sized pond stocked with carp, golden orf, and tench, two young beech trees by the eastern shore-side, and a flint-and-brick coal shed. The boys counted at least 15 fish in several minutes! The property's greenhouse backed onto a fenced cornfield (cornfield meaning wheat, oats, or any grain), which was also part of the estate.

The Duke's mother and sister lived in the great house adjacent to the church, Mrs. Cameron said. "You might see him driving through the village during racing season next September in his silver Jaguar. He's a real blue-blooded Duke, not some Johnnie-come-lately—lives in Scotland mostly, WWII hero, full head of silvery gray hair, very dashing."

We happily gave up grandmotherly advice to layer and wear wool all winter. The house had central heating and five coal burning fireplaces. The kitchen had a dishwasher and garbage disposal (unprecedented appliances in village houses back then). The larder was filled with shelving and an 18 cubic foot freezer—luxury of luxuries! Stocking the freezer and 'washing up' would be a piece of cake, and allow me to ditch those electricity converters we'd more or less inherited from the base resale store.

The laundry room had a washer, dryer, and old well pump that kept our vegetable garden alive and happy during the following summer's drought. We guessed correctly that the room's enclosed

8

W.C., a Burlington toilet with a pull chain, had once been outdoors—one amazing feature after another, and the best was yet to come!

The laundry room door opened to the back garden (a living illustration of a Gertrude Jekyll portrait)—full of daffodils popping up willy-nilly, like yellow spring fairies in the grass, bluebells clustered along the greenhouse wall, and a grand lilac nearly hiding the tool shed, it's burgundy-red blossoms thick and richly fragrant. David volunteered to mow the lawn if he could wait until the flowers were spent.

IV ~SETTLING IN ~

David claimed the attic room, one of four bedrooms. From the upstairs landing next to a fireplace and outside wall was an oak-cased door leading two flights up a narrow staircase to a rectangular bedroom with built-in bunks and a small dormer window overlooking the garden. The room's triangular pitch became a slight problem as David grew one and a half feet in two years. Tom argued he should have the room since he was the only one besides me who could stand up straight without bonking his head.

A majority of the original plaster separating the rooms had been removed in the house leaving exposed, original hand-hewn, vertical oak beams— giving the feeling of enlarged openness. In the living room, dining room, and what Mrs. Cameron called the reception hall (in spite of cold brick floors), the fireplaces and antiques Brian left made the rooms feel cozy.

Under the double-flight staircase the built-in bookcases were filled with enough good reading to teach English Lit. For starters Anthony Trollope, George Eliot, Thomas Hardy, Virginia Woolf, and Oscar Wilde's complete works.

The guestroom was both heavily used and haunted. That's right! This unbridled truth came straight from the mouths of the two Drake brothers, men then in their sixties who were born and raised in Ivy House, and whose family had sold the farm to Brian (or the cash investor, Brian's father).

10

We could count on the Drakes entertaining our houseguests with Ivy House ghost stories. They owned Musk's in Newmarket—Purveyors of Sausage to the Queen Mother, her royal crest hanging proudly outside the market's door. Considering her longevity we may have done ourselves a turn—the sausage was tasty.

Drake ghost stories varied slightly, but their delight in telling made for great sport. The house seemed to verify even the most skeptical among our friends and family, especially if the night wind was from the NE. Hundred-year-old oak sapling branches were woven in between a plaster of mud and limestone that made those old branches stretch and groan around the windows and doors—none the same size. The duct tape Wes applied to the spaces under the doorframes increased the eerie, sub-human sounds heard at times, especially when the kids were in bed and I was downstairs alone. I gave up Joyce Carol Oats for good on one of those nights.

Our friend Julie had just been through a difficult divorce when she arrived from Portland. She hadn't been to Western Europe before. Excited as she was about her two-week visit, she was apprehensive about being left on her own at all. The day after her arrival we took a short drive to see Ely Cathedral. On the way home through Newmarket, I stopped by Musk's to buy some lamb chops.

"I'd like you to meet my friend from Oregon," I said, introducing Julie to the Drakes, who were covered from head to toe in white starched aprons that almost touched the sawdust floor.

"Which room did they put you up in?" Will asked, frowning and running the edge of his knife back and forth on a butcher-block.

"Not across from the fireplace landing, I hope." I hadn't warned Julie about the ghost. I'd just told her the Drakes were previous owners of Ivy House. She hesitated.

"Well, I hung up my clothes and slept there last night," she said. Will checked his watch.

"Two days till the full moon. If you've got earplugs, you might want to stick them in this Thursday. If that wind whips up from the northeast, that's when she shows up holding onto that doll like it's a live baby girl. Lookin' out the window for that no–good womanizer," he said.

"She's a harmless ghost," Nigel said. "Don't go scarin' off our new American friends will ye now."

Dear Mother and Dad,   *June 12th, 1975*

Julie arrived before our furniture, which is just as well since I'd feel torn between getting settled and being a tour guide. The landlord left enough stuff for us to get along, and the guestroom is completely furnished. We borrowed pots and pans, etc., from the Base—thank heavens for hamburger helper!

I'm taking her to Stratford to see Othello, and with my trusty guidebook, "Turn Left at the Pub," we will spend a few days touring in the Cotswolds. You won't believe this house, especially the bathroom...

To say Brian and "his blokes" went all out on the upstairs bathroom is an understatement. I quote Airman 1st Class William Washington from Trenton New Jersey, the most dapper dresser at our first Christmas party, on seeing the bathroom, "Man, this here is dynamite!"

William wore a flared from the waist, light purple, ankle length coat and shiny cordovan boots that touched the hem. His coat almost got caught in a banister slat when he skipped a few steps going down the stairway.

As far as I remember, William's praise was echoed by every single one of our guests, including a friend from Eugene who asked to be photographed in *The Thinker* position while sitting on the commode, which was surrounded by polished Honduran mahogany. With the lid down the toilet looked like a built-in bench minus cushions. The same mahogany enclosed all sides of the room's six-foot bathtub (smack-dab in the middle and large enough for both Victoria and Albert).

A triptych mirror was centered over the Italian marble dressing table countertops with storage cupboards behind. There were shelves on either side of the sink— cubbyholes for all five of us and one to spare. The caramel-colored, plush wool, wall-to-wall carpet matched the marble counter tops, and that's not all! In one corner was a large tiled shower with a mahogany door and hinged-lidded clothes box for dirty linens. The opposite corner had a small cast iron, Victorian fireplace that actually worked. Mike, a bachelor flight surgeon who worked with Wes, suggested we invite a select few to our next party and hold it in the throne room.

We still exchange Christmas cards with the Fentons, the British couple that bought Ivy House after we moved. On a visit several years later I was staying with friends in Stetchworth. We were invited to Ivy House for tea. Eleven-year-old Alexandria Fenton asked if I had seen their baath room. "It was featured in *Country Life* three months ago, you see," she said.

Ivy House Front

Tom, Dave, and Doug

Back of Ivy House; Dave, Tom, and Doug

Off to Bottisham Village College

Newmarket; Horses Crossing the A-11

Patty with the Joys at Sandringham, Norfolk

North Yorkshire Moors; Tom and Bev Grassman

The Algarve, Portugal

Dear Mother and Dad,   *June 24th, 1975*

I tacked a card on the Post Office board to find cleaning help and presto, Mrs. Joan Mould, my new right arm! She was the second local caller I had last week. We agreed she'll come once a week for four hours, or as needed, plus she offered the services of her husband, Albert, to help in the garden—we'll see. So far David wants to mow the lawn and has taken over in the greenhouse. He's started enough tomatoes to supply a battalion, three kinds of lettuce, some onions and radishes, and sunflowers for the birds.

My second caller—a beady-eyed man with a husky, nasal brogue, knocked at the door to offer his services as my Turf Accountant. He was shorter than me, had on a tweed cap, unmatched coat and bow tie, and smelled like wet tobacco. I gathered he placed racing bets on horses throughout the UK, not just Newmarket, although he said his specialty was local. Wes offered to serve as my bookie if I was really into horse racing. I saved his card just in case...

If it hadn't been for the boys and Mrs. Mould, I doubt we'd have gotten beyond the 'good morning's, lovely day isn't it's,' and hat tipping by the villagers. Mrs. Mould was born and raised in a cottage between Stetchworth and Dullingham, lived her entire life in the village, and "began service with Lady Ellsworth (the Duke's mother) at about sixteen." There were other Ellsworth's close-by, she told me, but she always worked in the big house. She seemed to know everyone!

I asked Joan (she said to call her Joan) about the ambulance and medics I'd seen carrying a stretcher out of the house across the street. James Stetson's mother had died. She'd lived with the Stetson's for eight years.

"Will she have a service here?" I asked.

"She was new. I don't reckon anyone knew her that well," Joan said. So much for us, I'd thought at the time.

The pond was a favorite hangout for the village lads—providing built-in friends for the boys, especially Tom and David. On our arrival the matted, well-worn grass around three sides of the pond showed signs of recent use. Voila! No sooner had we set foot in the door than Phillip and Chris Robinson appeared—their poles and bait close behind. In a week's time, Doug and David Day, Nigel Hurrell, and the Robinson's were all in our kitchen making popcorn and "American" milkshakes.

Our electric blender was quite a curiosity. With the addition of ice cream and sauces of various flavors, milk, and sometimes bananas, our Osterizer produced something new and wonderful in their lives. English milkshakes didn't contain ice cream back then. They were more like whipped milk with added flavoring.

I've avoided telling the worst until now. We inherited a killer cat with Ivy House. It was fast and strong enough to leave one of the Duke's pheasants as a gift, placed squarely on the back porch mat. We couldn't open the screen without stepping on the beautiful bird, her head nearly severed from her long neck. Practically every morning Jack the Ripper, an outdoor tabby more bobcat than farm pet size, left a blue tit, robin, or field mouse on the mat along side the milk box and The London Times—shades of Rosemary's Baby.

Blue tits were Jack's specialty. Each morning after the milkman deposited the number of quarts we'd ordered, one at a time, the tits would peck through the foil tops to get at the first layer of cream (perfect set-up for Jack). Every single bird he caught was cornered and covered by two sides of porch and the roof. I'm a bird lover who doesn't mind cats, but Jack had had it!

"Take him to the pound, the cat crematorium, the Thames, I don't care, just get rid of him," I told Wes. I'm sure Tom didn't mind. He felt sorry for all the dead birds he'd collected. I'd given him the job of digging a hole in the field on the other side of the greenhouse to bury the birds, minus the pheasant that ended up on the Mould's dinner table. Sadly he'd buried them, or so I thought.

There may be more bird-loving birders in Britain than any country in the world per capita. At least that's the way it seemed on the day Reg Robertson rang up to ask if he could stop by with visiting cousins from Hampstead. It must have been September of that first year. I'd met Reg and his wife Phyllis at an on-going Cambridge Shakespeare class, and had invited all eighteen members to Ivy House for hamburgers and American beer on the 4th of July. Since that Fourth, several members had called on us during their Sunday drives.

I have no idea how many dead birds Tom had simply tossed over the fence in a pile, or how many flies were buzzing and skirting the edge of that dry cornfield, but the shrieks Reg's two cousins let out must have alarmed the entire village. Tom wished they'd left their binoculars in the car, "because I really caught it," he said. "I had to climb over and pick their binoculars up in the middle of that bird mess with my bare hands. Those people made scary faces at me. They acted like I was the killer, not Jack."

Mrs. Cameron said the milkman had been a prisoner of war in Japan, and never had much to say. He stopped by one morning when the Ripper was long gone.

"That was one mean cat. Steered clear of 'em," he said, straightening his tie. Then he added, "I'm wondering if you'd like to be knocked up when I'm carrying Stilton on the cart," he said in a soft monotone. I stifled a laugh, thinking, Wes won't believe this one.

"If Stilton's anything like Roquefort, I know my husband would like that very much," I said, thanking him.

After Jack, I'd almost decided it should be a permanent pet time out during our remaining years in England. In Portland and later

Eugene, we'd always had a dog or a cat plus various caged-type critters like guinea pigs, hamsters, and rats. I don't count guppies and goldfish since they never seemed to live long under my charge. But as luck would have it I met Anne Wakelam, my traveling hairdresser and soon- to-be good friend.

Anne's name came up when I called for a hair appointment at a Newmarket salon. After several visits there, she mentioned that she was going into business for herself. If I was interested she'd come to Ivy House and do my hair. Perfect! She ended up cutting the boys' hair as well.

It never ceased to amaze me how much stuff the English could fit into their small, fuel-efficient cars. Anne was an expert. She'd pull into the drive in her red Austin-mini and unload her tools of trade, including a hooded dryer and plastic shoulder drapes. All I provided were towels.

I guessed that most people born and raised in a horse-breeding, farming area like Newmarket were animal lovers. That observation was correct when it came to Anne and her husband Robin. He worked for the British Bloodstock Corporation and made his living transporting horses throughout the world. With a veterinarian brother and a very soft heart, it was easy for Anne to collect animals.

When I first saw the large fenced garden behind the Wakelam's lovely cottage in Isleham (a small village between Lakenheath and Newmarket), I counted three dogs. A corgi, a black lab, a collie, and several cats (including Topcat) a pregnant, coal-black longhair with a silky-white neck-piece and bowtie markings.

23

The first time the boys were scheduled for haircuts, Anne arrived early and asked Tom to come out to her car and lend a hand. Tom came racing back into the kitchen carrying a quilt-lined wicker basket with two of Topcat's twins—adorable, shiny-black kittens with their mom's soft white chin markings.

"Anne says they're free. Please can we have them, pleea-se," Tom said. In those days people didn't fly around the world with their animals in tow unless they were movie stars, presidents, or otherwise V.I. Ps. Since Wes and I didn't fall into any of those categories, I worried about what would happen to the cats when it came time to leave England. Anne promised she would find them a new home or keep them herself. *Could I resist?*

When Huntley and Brinkley were about eight weeks old, Wes gave a paper at a medical meeting in Garmisch, Germany. We decided to take some extra days and tour Normandy on our way home. While we were gone, Suzie, a corpsman who worked for Wes, stayed with the boys. Tom answered when I called home to see how things were going.

"Do you want the good news or the bad news first?" he said.

"How about the good news?"

"We didn't break any dishes, but the bad news is really bad," Tom said. "Huntley got run over in the High Street and the babysitter wrecked the Morris Minor on our way home from school."

"Did anyone get hurt?" I said, ready to cry.

"Nope," Tom said. "You know that big post at the railroad crossing? Suzie didn't make the curve and smashed up the front of the car. We had to walk about a mile in the pouring rain to get home."

"We had a proper funeral," David said when we got back. "We covered a wooden cross with honeysuckle vine and put dirt and grass over his grave. It's behind the greenhouse if you want to go look."

VIII ~BOYS AND BIKING ~

Doug spent his sophomore and junior years of high school at Colorado Rocky Mountain School (CRMS), a boarding school that focused on independent thinking, outdoors-man-ship, and scholastic excellence. Those two years helped get his teenage, risk-taking streak back on track.

Right after we moved to England, Wes bought Doug and David handmade bikes. Doug got busy planning a week-long trip of about 500 miles from the western tip of Cornwall along the West coast, with overnight stays at youth hostels— across Oxfordshire, through Bedford-shire, and back home. A major undertaking to say the least! It didn't take much arm-twisting for Doug to talk David into going along. I wasn't comfortable with the idea. They seemed too young, especially David. Wes was sure they'd do just fine.

We decided to take a family overnight trip to London, see *Mousetrap*, stay in a walk-up hotel near Paddington Station, and put the older boys on the train for Penzance with their bikes the following morning. At least we would see them safely through London and onto a south bound train . Fortunately Wes was the one to answer the phone the following Tuesday at dinner.

"David had an accident," Doug said, his voice cracking. "He's scratched up and bruised a bit. He totaled his Claude Butler."

David version was; "I was going down a long steep hill trying to keep sight of Doug. I let the brake off going about 60, missed the right curve and went flying headfirst into a thick hedgerow full of thorns. My face got all scratched up. It's a wonder I didn't poke my eyes out."

He landed next to the farmhouse of two very kind, elderly sisters who "filled a porcelain bowl with warm water and some analgesic-eucalyptus smelling stuff" to clean his scratched face and palms. On the phone the sisters insisted the boys weren't a problem. They wanted very much to help.

I don't remember their names, but what these angels did for our sons must have earned them a place in heaven. They made them dinner, put them up overnight, and had their hired man take David and his broken bike to the train the following day for home. Plus they let Doug use the telephone to rearrange hostel plans. No small feat!

The postal system in England was fast and far more efficient than in the US back then, but figuring out how to repay phone costs required wizardry. Every single telephone call had a different charge depending on where you were in the country, the destination of the call, and how long you spoke. So, included with our thank you we tried to reimburse their expenses—but then how could one possibly repay a pair of angels?

Doug arrived home about four days later. He said he'd met some interesting guys from Germany in the youth hostel, and rode two days with them. He told them we could put them up in Stetchworth. Swell Doug. He would be away kayaking. I was a slow learner, but that's when I drew the line. It finally dawned on me that young people who were mature enough to travel alone in a foreign country weren't the least bit shy about glomming onto a name, any name, to get a free meal and place to sleep.

First there was the sister of one of David's junior high friends. We'd never met the girl and didn't recognize the name when she called from London to ask whether she should take the train or hire a taxi to come see us in Stetchworth. She'd been in London for one night, seen Karl Marx's grave, and that was it for Ben Johnson's city. Then there was our goddaughter's boyfriend from Boston. He'd made it as far as Cambridge, and could we pick him up or tell him where to catch the bus to Stetchworth?

After that I got faster on the intake and issued the boys an ultimatum: "Your friends are welcome if you are here to entertain them. I'm not running a B&B and taxi service!"

We bought our Volvo station wagon with a left-hand drive shortly after moving to Stetchworth. We planned to ship it back to the states. I don't know how I could have managed without that car. It wasn't as bad as the 'Yank tanks' some Americans drove! Twice a month I'd shop at the base commissary to stock the cupboards, larder shelves, and freezer with peanut butter, canned soup, ice cream, chocolate chips, ranch dressing, frozen orange juice, canned tuna, cheerios, and taco shells—all the stuff that our boys had been used to back home. The car would be filled with food bags minus the fresh produce, meats, and breads I'd buy two or three times a week in Newmarket, Cambridge, or in a nearby village on market day.

We still get together with Berit and Svein Milford, our close friends from Bergen, Norway. Each time we do, the four of us have a good laugh over one of their visits to Ivy House. The Milfords lived in Eugene when Svein was a graduate business student at the University of Oregon. Among other things, Berit learned to love American canned tuna.

"I wish I could get your canned tuna in Bergen," she told me when they were getting ready to leave.

"Help yourself to as many tins as you'd like," I said. There must have been a dozen or more stacked next to the cat food—not too smart!

"Taking canned tuna to a country surrounded by ocean is a dumb idea," Wes said.

When Svein indicated he wasn't willing to carry home a bag full of canned fish, I winked at Berit, nodding toward the larder.

Berit said she couldn't keep a straight face when Svein was unloading their car in Bergen, grumbling about the weight of her suitcase. Svein said he couldn't keep a straight face when she opened the first can of cat food and realized her mistake.

Our friendship with Berit and Svein has enriched our lives over the years. In Eugene they baby-sat our sons when we were away. We skied together and shared many holidays, including a favorite July 4th at Crescent Lake, in 1980, when their son Thomas was ten, and his sister Anna was seven. They were like a second family to us all.

Thomas was 1 ½ on our first trip to Norway in 1973. Berit's parents kept him while we four adults had a grand tour of western Norway—up the coast, across the mountains at Voss and Vik, and finally to Hen where we met Wes' great-aunt Martha. She commented that Wes looked more Norwegian than our handsome young interpreter, Svein. In Oslo there were more of Wes' cousins to visit and eat with, take pictures and laugh with, and visit and eat with some more. Norwegians are warm and wonderful folks!

I was delighted when Berit called from London after a shopping trip to see if by chance we'd be home. What timing! We had five tickets to Swan Lake at Covenant Garden on Saturday—

which meant we had one extra, since Doug wasn't able to go. Dame Margot Fonteyn and Rudolph Nureyev were dancing. We were sitting in the lap of culture and I wanted the boys' introduction to ballet to be the best. Sharing it with Berit made that day even better.

Wes and I had seen Swan Lake several times, but never so magnificently done in such beautiful surroundings. All five of us were thrilled with the performance, but David's comment was worth the price of admission.

"Thanks Mom and Dad. If all ballet is like this, I wouldn't mind going again."

One of Doug's former instructors from CRMS was teaching in Northern Wales. That first August he invited Doug to help with kayaking classes and camp council, as well as entering an international ocean kayaking contest with him. They were the only American team represented. So off Doug went on his own, taking the train through Crewe and Chester to Colwyn Bay. He had a great time and his showmanship needs appeared to have been answered in spite of the fact that he and his former teacher came in last.

I found *The Treasures of Ireland* at the base library—a great book with detailed maps of places to hike and fish as well as historical stuff and touring details. Off we went with Tom and David to Ireland for two weeks.

We ferried from Holyhead to Dublin, spent our first night there, then headed northwest the following morning to look for the first Cairn (piles of stones about 4,500 years old) that marked Gaelic tombs. We may have set a record, climbing hills, checking out the huge ancient tombstones covering entrances (portal dolmens), and dodging more cow pies to check out Druid grave markers (ogam stones) than anyone before us.

The oldest Christian church in Ireland (between 5th and 6th C.) resembled an igloo, made out of stone rather than ice. It was small, compact, and windowless. My book said the church was maintained by local friars. Tom asked what a friar was.

"They made the first French fries," David told him. "See those grease spots on the road? They've been cooking around here for ages."

We soon learned that GB license plates were not a popular item in southern Ireland. When David was learning to drive, Wes claimed GB stood for Getting Better. In Ireland it might have meant Go Back home.

We drove by one farmhouse at least four times. According to my map the fenced field next door was full of ogam stones. I saw folks looking out the window at us. Against Wes' better judgment, I opened the gate of their picket fence, walked gingerly to the front door and knocked.

"I'm sorry to bother you. Are there ancient grave markers in the field over there?" I asked, smiling at a ruddy-faced woman who looked exactly like the first Betty Crocker, only scowling.

"Are you Americans?" she said.

"Yes we are. This is our first trip to Ireland. We've been hunting for old burial stones with our sons. My book shows they should be just over there."

"They are indeed," she said, smiling and nodding. "Would you all like a cup of tea before my husband shows you where to find the fence gate?"

It was raining when we visited the refurbished castle-home of William Butler Yeats, located on a pretty creek not too from Sligo. Tom stayed outside to skip rocks. I bought a small illustration:

And walk among long dappled grass,
And pluck till time and times are done
The silver apples of the moon,
The golden apples of the sun.

"This is such a dark place," our voracious reader David said. "I bet he didn't write that poem here."

Our most memorable night in Ireland was spent at a motel near Sligo Bay, close to the Northern border. There was a large campground on the beach with tent camps and a few caravans. After dinner the boys were itching to get back to the room to see television—for the first time in a week. Wes and I wandered outside to watch the sunset and family groups playing on the beach.

Music began wafting from the bar. One by one entire families meandered inside—toddlers to teenagers, parents to grandparents— some at tables, some on the floor. As many as possible were clustered around a small crusty woman at the piano. She had an up-swept ginger hair-do, a cigarette hanging out of the corner of her mouth, and fingers that flew back and forth across the keyboard, light as a butterfly. Like birdsong at sunrise, everyone began to join in…*It's a Long Way to Tipperary, Billy Boy, My Wild Irish Rose…* I left just long enough to pry the boys away from TV. "You'll love what's happening in the bar," I said as the three of us hurried down the hall toward the music.

On our next-to-last morning in Ireland, Wes took the boys fishing. I signed up for a mini-coach ride around "The Ring of Kerry," a circular drive of about 100 miles from Dingle Bay and around its southern peninsula to the Kenmare River. We wound through a mountain range know as Macgillicuddy's Reeks where subtropical vegetation seemed to flourish—fuchsia hedges, strawberry trees, even ferns and mosses in sheltered spots. The weather was perfect.

Our group of eight—seven passengers and the guide/driver— seemed pretty compatible except for the two guys in back who were obviously nursing a hangover. We headed south from Killarney at 10 a.m. on the dot, passed by Lough Leane to our left where the shadowy morning pines gave the lough a sinister look, and stopped at a roadside pub. It was 10:30.

Seamus, our jovial, robust, red-faced guide was a family man (eight kids) who did this run six days a week from April through September.

"We'll take a short, half-hour rest for those who need a break," he said, swinging the back doors open first so the sickish guys could air out. I walked over to the view with a young, in-love couple from Dublin, about Doug's age. The scene was spectacular.

The other passengers, two thirtyish German women in sweats, used their time to stretch and flex, and run in place. They looked like professional athletes. By the end of the day I learned that their much older husbands (or whatever) had several hotels near Cork that catered to Germans. "Lots of night work," they said.

About 10:45 I went inside to use the loo. When I came out Seamus motioned me toward the bar where the two guys sat with near-empty beer mugs and cloudy shot-glasses.

"This lady's an American. Her husband and sons have gone fishing for the day," he said, introducing me to the bartender.

We stopped at noon for lunch, and at three more pubs before returning to Killarney. Each time I went inside, Seamus introduced me to the bartender with the same explanation about my family off fishing. Since I'd had the bucket seat next to him, it dawned on me—he wanted everyone to know I was a paying passenger. Close to Kenmare I pointed out that Wes and the boys had just passed us. He seemed relieved, like I'd made an honest man out of him. Perhaps women weren't supposed to be vacationing about alone in 1975 Ireland.

The talk in Stetchworth that first August was of a famous author and his wife who'd bought the Georgian house across the High Street from us, next to Stetson's. Undoubtedly our soon-to-be neighbors were told about the American officer's family who'd moved in across the street. We were lucky to be in Stetchworth, where we as newcomers began a fast friendship with Edward and Emily Joy.

Surrounded by grazing sheep and lazy Suffolk cornfields, neo-classical Ickworth House appeared as a mirage the first time I saw it. Ickworth's three-story rotunda loomed above the fog like a Homeric ghost. The stately home was built about three hundred years ago to house the spoils of Frederick Hervey's continental tours. This 4th Earl of Bristol/ Bishop of Derry traveled big time. He collected paintings by Titian, Velasquez, and Gainsborough, 18th century French and English furniture, and lots of silver. Edward Joy's expertise was perfect for his role as curator of Ickworth House. Edward's epitaph in Cambridge, 'And gladly wolde he lerne, and gladly teche,' describes him to a T.

Our first invitation for drinks before Sunday dinner might have been our last. Wes did enjoy an occasional martini! Both of us were of the 'never before five' mentality, so when Edward amicably asked what I'd like to drink, I decided sipping a glass of sherry was a safe bet.

"I'm having a gin," Emily said, when Wes asked what others had ordered.

"I'll have a gin too," Wes said, expecting it over ice. Edward gave him a crystal highball glass, half full and neat. Wobbling across the street afterward, Wes complained about a good way to waste a Sunday afternoon. I told him I was sure they didn't expect him to have a refill!

Edward was a tall, erect, powerful-looking man. I'd watch him 'walking briskly to post' from my kitchen window just before nine a.m., the tip of his cap above his thick, dark eyebrows tilted skyward—looking toward the calling doves, assessing the cumulus clouds, breathing the honeysuckle-scented air. Edward had been a Principal Lecturer in History at London University, an internationally acclaimed authority on English furniture, and the author of seven books— with several more in the works when we met him.

Emily was the typical Englishwoman-gardener, often outside pottering (her term) with a perfect eye for design and color, a knowledge of plants that included every single botanical name. Impressive! Her round sparkling eyes were full of interest, humor, and a touch of stubborn grace—another Taurus like me, the stubborn part maybe?

"The easy thing about gardening," she said after we'd met, scraping mud from her boots with the shovel she'd used to transplant a healthy start of a sweet-scented rambler 'Goldfinch' next to a cream-colored clematis climbing the garden's gate (I was learning), "If a plant isn't happy in it's location, simply move it," Emily said.

Wes still rues the day she told me that!

The Joys were a well traveled couple—to Africa when their daughter Ruth and her husband lived in Tanzania, to the U.S. and Canada with Edward as furniture historian and lecturer, and throughout the British Isles, Russia, and Western Europe. They were open to new experiences and had sophisticated food tastes. In spite of all the above, tacos, enchiladas, chili rellenos, and guacamole wouldn't have been my first menu choice when I asked them and their daughter Alison and family to dinner.

"Let's have Mexican food," Tom said. He was sure his new friend Patrick Barnes (the Joys' grandson) would like it. Neither the Barnes' nor the Joys' had eaten Mexican food before, but it seemed to have been a hit—counting the number of thank you's and the amount consumed.

Tom demonstrated how to pick up and eat tacos with one's hands. Patrick followed suit. The others wisely stayed with their knives and forks.

Every Christmas I pull up Emily's handwritten Yorkshire Pudding recipe. Unfortunately it never comes out like hers.

Yorkshire pudding for four

largely a matter of trial and error
1-1/2 to 2 oz plain flour
1 large egg
about 2 tablespoonfuls milk
"   1   "   water

I have found most recipes unhelpful and always recommending too much flour. Sieve flour into basin & break egg into it. Work egg into flour with wooden spoon & add milk gradually. Beat well either with spoon or mixer for at least five minutes.

Here comes the confusing part! Cover and leave to stand in cool place for 20 minutes or as long as you like. Add water. Then pour into pie dish which has been lightly greased with fat from under the joint. Bake on top shelf at 400 or 425 for 15 to 20 minutes. I'm sorry to be a bit vague but a lot depends on the flour & the oven. When the egg and milk have been added the mixture should look like thick cream, & with water it should look like thin cream. Good luck!

By now you've figured out that I'm a died-in-the-wool anglophile. My addiction became serious on our first visit to Cambridge in 1975. At the time we were still living in base housing. We collected my Aunt Kathryn and Uncle Don from the train station, joined a walking tour at the Tourist Information Center, and after several blocks decided to go it alone, my trusty "Turn Left at the Pub" guide in hand. David's first impression mirrored my own.

Dear Grandma and Grandpa,   *June, 1975*

How are you? I'm just great. England is very green and beautiful. It's really old and interesting—nothing like Longview and Eugene. Have you heard of Cambridge? It's famous for its Colleges. We met Aunt Kathryn and Uncle Don here and went to see Kings College.

It has this painting by Peter Paul Rubens, "Adoration of the Magi." It was probably the most impressive thing I've ever seen. I know you'd both like it. It's the most valuable painting in the world. It is insured for $7,000,000. We're going to a pub for lunch—they let kids in taverns in England...

Come and see us. Love, David

We left the tour at Kings College to catch our breath. The lawns beside the Cam River were set with willow trees and views of the riverside colleges and their sweeping backs—perfect photo ops! The organ was playing a Bach cantata as we entered the chapel.

Nothing could have prepared me for the sudden chill or the tremor I felt. As the music swelled I looked up at the magnificent fan-vaulted ceiling—a trumpeting angel atop the organ. My heart skipped a few beats. *Could the gates of heaven be like this?* It's the closest I've come to what I've heard described as a religious awakening. How could a 15th Century building hold me in such awe?

During the summer months Cambridge was so crowded with visiting students and tour groups from all over the world that we steered as clear as possible. The other nine months were a different story. Once a month there were contemporary and classical performances at the Arts Theatre, the boys choir at Kings College Chapel each Sunday, and punts to rent by the hour on the Cam River. With a partner seated in the middle, our visitors loved to stand in the back of the punt on a platform, dig the pole in the shallow river bottom, and push. The punt simply slid down river as the scenery rolled by.

Cambridge offered every venue of adult education, from hobby classes to the study of Medieval Art and Architecture. On a trip to Yorkshire and the North during spring vacation, I dragged David, Tom, and our friends to Durham to see the Cathedral, the final resting place of St. Cuthburt. I'd written a paper on that oppressive Norman fortress for the Medieval Architecture Class. Actually the kids were mesmerized by the bizarre story of monks carrying Cuthburt's remains up and down Northumbria, and evading waves of marauding Danes in a chase that lasted 120 years. Durham was a bigger hit than Hadrian's Wall—more on that later.

Each of the many times I drove to Cambridge, I'd get behind the steering wheel and seem to automatically pull SW out of my driveway, drive through Six-Mile Bottom by Swynford Paddocks, now a hotel and fancy restaurant, but once the home of Augusta Leigh, Lord Byron's cousin and sometimes mistress. Then to Trinity College Library to gape at Byron's life-sized marble statue and wonder about the handsome poet who rode horseback over those same flat roads.

Trinity Library is a vast hall with bookshelves lining the walls beneath the windows and at right angles to form a series of bays filled with student study tables. In the center are glass-enclosed viewing tables containing rotating manuscripts from the school's famous alumni—John Milton, Charles Dickens, and A.A. Milne's autographed manuscript of Winnie the Pooh to name a few.

I memorized the college's opening hours and like a sponge, I'd fill myself a day at a time with as much as I could soak in before the kids got home from school. In spring and summer the gardens of Queens and Clare Colleges were magnets—English lavender lined both sides of the entrance to Clare in billowing light purple and sage, lush and thick and perfectly rounded. On a gray day I'd take in Emanuel College where John Harvard tried to spread the word that beauty is sinful, and then that good Puritan took off for America— I'll pass on that topic.

I thank my friend Ginny Starr for telling me about the History of London class offered at Fulham and South Kensington Institute. Every Wednesday morning at 7:45 during that first school year, off I'd go to Dullingham, park the car, and board the train to Cambridge (a ten minute ride), then transfer to London/Kings Cross. The underground (tube) from Kings Cross went across town to within a block of the Institute, housed in an unassuming two story brick building with a good-sized auditorium.

Promptly at 10:00 a.m., our teacher and London guide Peter Hazelton, would scan the room of some forty plus, pinch his raised chin and say, "Hmm, well now, it seems we have at least two brave men willing to scramble up the dome of St. Paul's and feast our eyes upon one of the most beautiful panoramas in London." Mr. Hazelton would then proceed to lecture with a slide presentation, giving us as much information as we could possibly absorb about the cathedral, or whatever the topic of study was that day. Armed with his marked instructions—which pubs en route had decent food and what tube to take we'd break at 11:30 and reconnoiter at 1:30 p.m., by the steps to the cathedral's west entrance.

Mr. Hazelton didn't have to carry a bright orange flag as he led us briskly through Pudding Lane toward Fish Street Hill, pausing to show us where, in 1666, the Great Fire of London began. His six foot three or four husky frame, dark green umbrella, and French beret did the trick. Besides, it was easier not to miss anything, dogging right on his heels.

Most people associate Hampton Court with Henry the VIII and Christopher Wren's amazing architecture. I relate it to the day

Tom got stuck in that palace garden's vast maze. He was on school holiday so I took him to London with me.

"Look up. Look up," Mr. Hazelton said in his booming baritone. "This is by far the most important suggestion I will make during our modest study of the world's finest city and surroundings, its art and architecture! There's great beauty to behold beyond the eye's level."

So while I was diligently studying the decorative gate's ironwork (the Tijou Screen) Tom decided to check out the maze. Next thing I heard was his American accent yelling "Hey Mom, how do I get out of here?"

Mr. Hazelton frowned at me, extended his dark green umbrellas as high as it would go and called out loudly, "Go straight west, laddie. Take the first left and look up toward my umbrella. The exit is just a hedge away."

"You're welcome to bring the lad along," he said, standing by the exit, his right arm holding the umbrella's extended staff, "Just keep him in tow from now on please so we can move right along."

The make-up of the class changed slightly each term. Except for the occasional drop-in male, it was strictly women— spouses of businessmen living abroad, diplomats, academics on sabbatical, military personnel—none British. My London companion Rachel's husband was an executive with Ford Motor Co. Ford Escorts were a big seller in the British Isles back then. Rachel lived in Luton, less than forty miles from Stetchworth, but getting there was like going to Portland from Eugene on a two to four-lane, A road—our friendship remained in London.

XIII ~EAST ANGLIA, HORSES, & THE AIR FORCE ~

One of Wes' jobs as a flight surgeon was a monthly sortie in an F-4, a two-seated jet where he learned to be a GIB, or guy-in-back (navigator). He loved these exciting flights over the UK, and to air bases in western Europe, and had great respect for the pilots he flew with. I tried not to think about what he was doing!

Squadron Commander Wayne Lehr was one of his first mentors. Early on Wayne's English wife Doreen and I became good friends and fellow members of The English Speaking Union. This offered me first-hand exposure to English culture.

The members of the local ESU were all East Anglicans except for those of us from RAF Lakenheath, Alconbury, and Mildenhall (mostly officers' wives). Most other members were retired military and foreign service people, local dignitaries, and a few titled gentry. The three or more American military bases in East Anglia provided jobs and other big boosts to the local economy. Eldon Griffith, MP, was an ESU member and local politician who knew his conservative constituency like his own mother. Mr. Griffith was a charmer, well educated, and nobody's dummy.

I dragged Wes to an ESU dinner at the Athenaeum in Bury St. Edmunds where Mr. Griffith was guest speaker.

Dear Mother and Dad,

I'm glad you told me 'when in Rome, do as Romans do.' I haven't gotten the words down to God Save the Queen yet, but knew enough to stand at attention.

We went to an English Speaking Union dinner in Bury with some 200 other members and guests. Wes was in his element, discussing politics with the local Member of Parliament over Chicken Marengo.

I'm having the ESU group meeting at Ivy House next month for coffee (eleven's). I'm told English people love to come to American homes and sample our cookies and cakes. No wonder. Their sweet biscuits remind me of the Lorna Dunes and Fig Newtons you used to try and get Larry and me to eat—we're talking filler...

Doreen Lehr swung by to pick me up the morning of the ESU meeting at Sir John Wedgwood's home. Doreen's a petite, blue-eyed, perfectly turned out blonde who designed and made most of her fashionably smart clothes—an artist with class-A talent. On that sunny May morning, the ESU members who'd already arrived were in the gardens. Doreen suggested checking out the Wedgwood collections before it got crowded in the house.

I thought the butler looked a bit tattered in his tweed jacket with leather elbow patches that even I could have sewn, in spite of the spit-polish on his shoes. His white shirt was stiffly starched, but frayed at the collar stay tips and on both sleeves. He had thick salt and pepper hair and bushy eyebrows—slightly disheveled looking for a servant, but then who was I to judge?

"Please do come in," he said, smiling rather roguishly, nodding to Doreen whose Oxford accent matched his perfectly. "Perhaps I'll have time to show you the collection rooms personally.

47

Let's see here." He mumbled something about starting with Catherine the Great. I was ready to file him into the eccentric category and carry on alone when Doreen looked at me, her eyes wide as a great horned owl, nodding to his back and mouthing, "Sir John."

I don't remember the flaw that he pointed out in the 100 piece set of china, returned by Empress Catherine some 175 years earlier. What I do remember was Sr. John's humble admiration for his great-great-grandfather, Josiah, "The finest of ceramic artists, who was the first to market Wedgwood wares to European aristocracy and commoners. Josiah set the family business a-sail for us to prosper and enjoy. A right jolly-good fellow, he."

XIV   ~HOUSES OF PARLIAMENT ~

In March before spring break, Eldon Griffith invited 20 RAF Lakenheath officers' wives to lunch at the Houses of Parliament Terrace Room overlooking the Thames—first come first serve. Brenda, the Wing Commander's wife, called me about the invitation. A coach (bus) had been hired to drive us to London and back. I was excited!   No one complained about the drizzle shrouding South London that day.   All I could think of were the famous MP's who had lunched there and maybe even warmed the very same seat— Clement Atlee, Margaret Thatcher, perhaps even Winston Churchill.

Mr. Griffith had just two tickets to the Strangers' Gallery in the House of Commons after lunch.   Brenda and General Rozencranz's wife got those, naturally.   The rest of us 'who were interested' could visit the 'sitting' House of Lords.'   Sitting struck me as an amusing term since half the Gothic hall of wigged and robed gentlemen were flat out sleeping.   The speaker kept droning on in a Scottish brogue that I had trouble catching, seemingly oblivious of his lazing audience.

When we got up to leave, a dark-complected, youngish man with a Tony Perkins face and build approached us.   He'd come in behind us and was sitting two rows above, obviously waiting for a chance to speak to us.

"Excuse me.   May I introduce myself," he said positioning his briefcase across the isle, making it difficult for us to pass.   "I'm an entrepreneur. If there's anything I can do for you whilst you're in London, I'm at your service."

We said no thank you and laughed all the way home, thinking up all kinds of services he might have provided, their cost, and how he planned to handle three women at a time.

Around Newmarket the rule of thumb was breeding beauties, racing winners, and in effect lionizing horses. The following is an example: Wes was the first member of an Air Force inspection team to arrive when an F1-11 crashed about 50 yards from a Newmarket elementary school—in session. The pilot and navigator ejected safely (the entire cockpit intact with the two men inside) and landed in the field of a local stud farm, rather close to a paddock. The second inspector on the scene was Eldon Griffith.

"It's a miracle the plane didn't crash into that school full of kids," Wes said.

"Thank God it didn't kill any horses," Mr. Griffith said. "There'd be hell to pay for sure!"

According to Wes, as the pilots climbed out of the standing cockpit, a sturdy lady resembling Mrs. Woodhouse of former PBS fame came striding across the field with a full tea tray. "I'm sure you chaps could use a cup of tea just now," she said. "You must be absolutely done in."

Anyone on the A45 and A12 from Cambridge/London on racing day knew that Newmarket wasn't just about breeding horses. To say the races at Newmarket drew a crowd is an understatement—

throngs were more like it. An AF pediatrician had introduced us to Mrs. Putnam, whose late husband was a member of the private Jockey Club in town. Better yet, her invitational tickets included access (as her guests) to the Members Enclosure at the track.

Years before I'd been to the dog races in Portland with an old boyfriend. We sat in the bleachers. That June day was my very first horserace and it was a doozy. The staging, the folderol, the glamour and accompanying excitement was real!

Mrs. Putnam was partial to Americans, especially those with titles or a rank above Captain. When she called to invite us to the race I mentioned that we had a young fellow staying with us, a Stanford student who'd recently finished an exchange in Germany.

"Stanford is one of your better universities, I've heard. Do bring him along. I'd love to meet him," she said. "It isn't necessary to wear a hat, although you'd be quite comfortable if you choose to do so."

I knew almost nothing about how to place a bet on a horserace even with the information provided on the racing form—like a horse's sire and whether it was a mudder (horses that do well in mud). On that particular day it might have been important. Most of the time I remember I spent gawking at the Queen's box—a fenced, gated, open-air enclosure that seated about twelve royals looking straight ahead or leaning an ear into the person next to them—or at the outrageous women's hats, or the oozing confidence of the jockeys in spite of their size, or in the tearoom drinking tea and deciding which of the sweets and savory sandwiches were the most tempting.

When it came to placing bets, Tom Atwood, Doug's visiting friend, saved the day. There were about six to nine races on a card, and 15 to 30 minutes between each race depending on how long it took to get the bets in on one's horse. That's where Tom Atwood came in. He'd collect our party's cards and betting money, race to the betting booth, and be back before you could say Jack Robinson. I'm sure he burned off all the calories he took in that day. Scarf seems like a strong word to use in describing the enthusiasm with which Tom entirely cleaned two large silver trays of goodies after the rest of us had finished, and in spite of the fact that Mrs. Putnam had said, "Just eat what you'd like dear and please leave the rest."

XV   ~OVERNIGHT TO BELGIUM~

One weekend not long before school started, Wes had to be involved in MASH-type practice maneuvers with the British, held in the Thetford Forest near Lakenheath. It was a perfect time for me to take the boys on an overnight trip to Belgium. The four of us drove to Felixstowe, parked the Volvo, and caught the overnight ferry to Ostende. I had reserved a four-bunk sleeper. You might have called it a four midget sleeper, en-suite. Tom and I could barely stretch out with our toes hanging over the bunk ends. Doug and David were doomed to rest in the fetal position, which may be the reason they stayed up most of the night playing the slots.

I didn't learn how little time they spent sleeping, or what they'd been up to, until an officious, puffy, pink-cheeked woman who looked like she'd been up all night herself approached me as we neared the Ostende dock.

"Your lads were having quite a time of it last night," she said in a meddlesome tone. "Perhaps they made enough to treat the little family to breakfast."

Doug and David were in bed when my alarm went off. The coach meeting us was already parked near the gangplank. I decided not to spoil our long day in Belgium by giving them the third degree or chewing them out right then. Miss Nosey grabbed the first seat directly behind the bus driver. Since we were on our own, I assumed she was too.

"Sit by the middle window half way back," I told the boys, hoping to get rid of her.

Our first stop was Brussels. True to description, the architecture was magnificent. We saw St. Michael's Cathedral and then went to the outdoor square overlooking the Palace. David spied fresh strawberries in the open market. Perfect with the hot chocolate and sweet rolls they'd consumed before I found any of the handmade lace coasters and hankies I wanted for gifts.

When we stopped to take pictures of the "Little Boy" fountain, guess who walked right behind us and on up the street? Spiro Agnew in the flesh, crew cut and all. My reputation for seeing celebrities was notorious in our family, so when I pointed Spiro out to the boys they must have said in unison, "Sure Mom!" With that he turned around. Sure enough—it was the former veep, smiling and nodding, probably all the way to the Brussels Bank.

Brugge is called the Venice of the North, and rightly so. It was drizzling by the time we took a boat ride through the city's canals. That didn't stop me from "looking up" and enjoying the city's touted 12th-14th century architecture that was apparently saved on purpose during the German occupation. To avoid Miss Nosey we ducked into one of what must have been the most expensive restaurants in Brugge for lunch. Unfortunately, I couldn't read the menu or the prices posted outside. After that experience I never forgot to pack our lunches before leaving home!

The last stop was Antwerp, Belgium's second-largest seaport. The ancient Guild houses lining the marketplace were well preserved. Even in a country rebuilt after WWII, I was impressed with the age of everything.   Peter Paul Reubens had lived and worked in Antwerp centuries earlier. We all decided the two Rubens paintings in the Cathedral of Notre Dame didn't hold a candle to "The Adoration of the Magi" at Kings College.

We were in our car by seven and home by nine p.m., making me wonder how long the ferry back-peddled on the way across the channel.   I decided I'd let Wes deal with Doug and David's gambling on the ferry crossing. Apparently it was legal for underage kids. Tom and I had gotten some sleep, and the older boys didn't seem worse for wear. I let them know they didn't get away with much. Besides, staying up all night might have been preferable to those tiny bunk beds.

XVI   ~WHAT'S IN A NAME~

From Cub Scouts through junior high, Randy Morrow had been David's best buddy. David had been looking forward to Randy's month-long summer visit, planning all the places they would go, and talking him up to his friends in the village.

"What is the lad's given name?" Joan Mould asked me.

"I think it's Randy," I said.

"Would his Christian name be Randall?" she asked. "I should think what you've called him would not be a proper name. It wouldn't be in this country."

That was in the days before Prince Andrew's nickname was a household joke. Joan wasn't about to speak Randy's name out loud. I was clueless. Was it because it wasn't a saint's name like Matthew, Mark, Luke, or John, I wondered? A Catholic friend had asked me what Doug's Christian name was, after we had called him Douglas Wesley. Had we been Catholic, we would have given him a saint's name.

Tom was happy to clear up the mystery that night at dinner.

"Chris and Phillip said randy is a dirty word. It means he does naughty stuff with girls," he said.

"That's enough Tom!" Wes said. David's cheeks looked like he'd spent the day in the sun.

"Nigel and the Robinsons have been teasing me about Randy's name. I'll just tell him when he gets here—we'll call him Morrow, or Ran. It'll be okay," David said. Subject dropped.

56

Wes and David went to Heathrow to meet Randy's plane. Wes decided to take a 45 minute detour on the way home and swing by Windsor Castle, an impressive edifice, even from the motorway. Wes told me that Randy and David talked non-stop in the back seat on their way home —about girls, fishing, soccer, everything from soup to nuts, without one glance out the window. As they neared the castle, Wes stopped at a lay-by.

"How come you're stopping?" David asked.

"I thought Randy might like to see Windsor. It's a pretty impressive castle," Wes said. Randy looked back over his shoulder without bothering to turn around.

"Nice, thanks," Randy said.

I opted to stay home on an unusually steamy Sunday when Wes took the boys to the Mildenhall Air Show. Wes has a love affair with airplanes, which seemed to spill over on Tom—not so Randy and David.

"You guys are going to love this show," Wes said at breakfast. "We'd better get an early start. It'll be crowded."

Everyone listened, sort of, as he told about the Harrier Jump Jet that takes off vertically or horizontally—the C5 Galaxy, the A10 Warthog, the SR 71 Blackbird.

"Every bloke in East Anglia, their wives and kids were lined up knee deep outside that chain length fence," Wes told me later. "Sitting on fenders, hoods—some brought folding chairs. It was hot!" David and Randy looked at each other and smiled—inside joke?

"I'm not sure either one of them looked skyward the entire time," Wed said later, half joking, part annoyed. "I know teenage boys have one-track minds, and the girls were definitely underdressed. Oh well, Tom liked the show. Better luck tomorrow in Cambridge."

I had errands to do that Monday in town, and planned to visit a friend while David took Randy punting on the Cam River. I lucked out and found a parking place on a busy street in front of Heffer's bookstore. I had on a culotte skirt that hit me mid-knee, a cotton sleeveless blouse, and sandals.

"Hop out," I said to Randy and David. "I'm going into Heffer's. Watch for me at the punt dock in about two hours."

"You're going shopping with that on?" David said, looking at my exposed knees. "You don't have to get out of the car when you come to pick us up, Mom. We'll find you."

XVII ~KAISERS & FARNES~

Our German friends Nancy and Kurt Kaiser and their son and daughter visited us one August on their way to vacation in Ireland. Nancy grew up in Baker City, went to OSU and the U of W, and excelled in languages. After graduation she worked as a translator for American Express in Berlin, married Kurt, and has lived in Southern Germany ever since.

That summer the weather was unseasonably warm in England. Ten-year-old Tom decided it would be fun to pitch a tent in the back yard and sleep outside with Thomas Kaiser, about seven.

We parents were sitting in the living room sipping some delicious Trockenbeeren Auslese dessert wine that the Kaisers brought as a house gift, when the two boys burst through the back door. Thomas Kaiser was crying. Our Tom gave me a bewildered look and shrugged his shoulders. Thomas Kaiser went directly to his mother, speaking a mile a minute in German. In between sobs I heard him say, "Thomas Jacobs," then more sobs and whimpers. Nancy tried to shush him, speaking softly in German.

"What's happened? Tell me what I can do to help," I said. "He'll be all right," Nancy said in English, which made him cry all the louder. All the while Kurt sat quietly scowling at his son.

"Thomas," I was told later Kurt had said in no uncertain terms, "Get up directly." Kurt then took hold of Thomas' arm and the two marched out the back door.

The tent idea was nixed and both boys reluctantly and for different reasons ended up inside, in Tom's bunk beds. It seems the problem began when Tom removed his high top Keds and socks inside the tent. In this case the skunk didn't smell his own smell first—and Thomas Kaiser couldn't get to sleep because, "Thomas Jacobs feet stink!"

It was late spring when our good friends from Portland, Sally and Dick Farnes, came to visit for a few days on their way to see the Kaisers in southern Germany. Sally and Nancy are sisters. We had fun touring around East Anglia with the Farnes, visiting Cambridge, and introducing them to the Drake Brothers in Newmarket, who commented that it was always safer to have two in a haunted room, and cautioned Dick to keep an eye on the Mrs. after dark.

On their last day I packed our cooler with a picnic lunch, threw a car robe in the trunk, and the three of us (Wes had to work) skirted London and headed south to Chartwell, the country home of Winston Churchill and a popular place with Americans because of all the WWII memorabilia. We were happily settled on a grassy knoll overlooking the rose garden, minding our own business, eating our sandwiches and waiting for the 2 o'clock opening when a tour coach unloaded close-by. It was full of Americans from New England or Boston, where every word ending in an a sounds like er (Americer, for example) and every word ending in er sounds like an a (sista, for sister).

A lady in lilac polyester pants and green sneakers jumped down the steps and ran toward us squealing "PRINGLES! Where on earth did you find PRINGLES! We've been in England for two weeks and I haven't seen one single box of Pringles. I luv em," she said with a Carol Channing rasp, practically falling all over us by now. I felt like every single person within a 50-foot radius was staring.

"I got these chips at an American commissary near-by," I said. "I doubt they sell them here yet, but you're welcome to the rest of these when we're done."

Sally Jo and Dick had a seven p.m. reservation on the Dover/Calais ferry to France. A photograph of the last stop I'd planned on our drive SE to the channel would have made a perfect cover for *In Britain* magazine. The sun was starting down to the west of Bodiam Castle, a flawless example of 14-century English architecture. It had never been attacked or marauded. A swan swimming in the moat made a v-shaped riffle on the water, the drawbridge was up, the turrets and fortified walls were empty and silent. We were too late to go inside but who cared? As we watched the sun fade behind a huge copper beech we stared at the perfect scene. Not bad. Not bad at all.

XVIII ~ FIRST SPRING BREAK~

That first spring break Doug went on a Lakenheath Senior Class trip to Majorca, Spain, while Wes was off on an exercise to Aviano, Italy, with Squadron Commander Jim Grassman. Jim's wife Bev and I decided it would be fun to take the other five kids north for the holiday.

In retrospect, since we hadn't traveled together before, I was more than overly optimistic about spring weather in Northern England (dumb is more like it). I figured if Bev could handle Tom's somewhat keyed activity level (when he was little his brothers called him hyper-diaper), and my tendency to over-program, we'd do just fine.

Bev had told me she'd planned to eke out any family times she could in England, with or without Jim. Squadron commander's wives had big time duties: wives' club meetings, entertaining, nurturing the younger, often homesick women—a role she filled with calm attention. Bev spoke slowly and looked directly at you with her dark, intense eyes. Her sensory antenna was built in. I wasn't surprised to learn she was part Navaho.

I'd met Jean James years ago through mutual friends in Portland, when Wes was in medical school and I was teaching second grade. After Jean's first husband died she returned to Gilling East, Yorkshire, married Rod James, a retired Naval Officer, and raised a second family. I was lucky we'd kept in touch.

On the first day we made it all the way from Suffolk to Yorkshire—to the B&B that Jean had arranged for us close to her home. We'd planned to stay three days. Jean invited our whole bunch for dinner those nights and encouraged us to stay even longer. In spite of the kids' pleas—they'd already spotted the James' paddock, horses, and good-sized riding ring—a little bell jangled my ear with Wes' Aunt Dorothy's saying: 'Visitors, like fish, begin to smell in three days.' I declined the offer.

"Anything to do with Yorkshire, Jean's an aficionado! She likes to pound the pavement," Rod James said that first night at dinner. He was referring to Jean's offer to take us touring around James Herriot's country— with an English woman's bent.

Like many girls their age, Gretchen and Wendy Grassman were avid equestrians. Bev said their "nutty enthusiasm" was inborn.

"If I allowed it they'd spend every waking minute around horses—mucking out, going on hacks, dressage, the whole bit." So, at the first mention of horses the girls were ready to pack their bags. Fourteen-year-old Jay wasn't as enthusiastic.

"Five kids in that station wagon?" he said. "Who's sitting way back?"

Before we left for York the next day, Jean told Bev and the girls they were welcome to stay at the house and ride, but that they wouldn't want to miss seeing Castle Howard (of *Brideshead Revisited*) and Rievaulx Abby the following day.

Jean and I took off mid-morning with David, Tom, and Jay.

"The boys will enjoy climbing and exploring York's 700 year -old city walls. While they're at the museum with fossils and Roman archaeological things, we'll slip over to Mayberry's near the Minster. It's my idea of the best china shop in the world...you'll love the Shambles too, (a medieval street) leading to it," she said.

When Rod heard what I'd bought (a set of everyday earthenware that I still use) he said, "My dear wife gets a cut with every buyer she introduces to Mayberry's."

"Go on, Rod. Someone might take you seriously," Jean said.

"Mom, there's no room for any more stuff in the back," Tom said, when he spotted the boxes. "You don't have to sit back here!"

The following day the eight of us squeezed into Jean's Land Rover and headed north through lightly wooded countryside toward Helmsley, a small market town at the base of the North York Moors.

"Each fall every room within a ten mile radius of Helmsley is booked. This little town bursts at the seams with hunters from around the globe," Jean said.

"What do they kill? Tom asked.

"Well they hunt edible birds. Partridge, chucker, quail, pheasant," she said.

"Our cat killed lots of birds but only one you could eat. Mom gave it away to this lady in Stetchworth—I mean the pheasant not the cat."

"Let's don't go into that, Tom," I said.

As Jean drove over a hill and the magnificent arches of the Rievaulx Abby choir came into view the kids said in unison, "Whooo! Cool!"

"What is this neat place?" Jay said.

"The abby is a monastic ruin founded by Cistercian Monks over 800 years ago. Did I hear cool? Believe me it gets pretty cold down there nine months of the year," Jean said.

We spent close to an hour climbing in and around the huge pillars, following Jean's guide book, trying to figure out where the Monks slept, ate, went to church, and washed.

At Castle Howard the boys opted to explore the grounds. Jean had been an occasional volunteer guide at the mansion. She hit the highlights with expertise: the long gallery and paintings by Reynolds, Gainsborough, and Holbein, the stables that had been converted to exhibit 17th through 20th century costumes, and the huge kitchen that the girls said reminded them of "Upstairs, Downstairs."

We got off to a late start that last day. We'd planned to stop at Barnard Castle where Tom was going to camp in August. Fortunately for all of us the castle was closed. When we piled out of the car and peered through the windy mist Wendy said,

"Might be fun if it's not raining."

Recently I asked Tom what he remembered about spending those two weeks in a castle. His only response was,

"Elvis Presley died."

The moors in spring were quite different than the banks of heather I'd pictured from reading "Wuthering Heights." We pulled over on a level grassy roadside area to eat the lunch Jean had packed. In every direction we saw squares of tended grass and hay, a few shrubs, and dry sage-scented heather surrounded by high flat plains. It was clear, jacket-weather with a light wind. A flock of the friendliest, pet-able, black-faced sheep kept the kids from driving us nuts, which they almost did rereading the B&B brochure aloud:

> *Visit Hadrian's Wall and ride horseback*
> *Near Alston by the River Tyne*
> *The Sutcliffe's Live & Let Live B&B*

Jean and Rod had suggested we see a few of their favorite places on the North Sea, including Robin Hood's Bay. Why oh why didn't I ask them what they thought about our B&B— The Live & Let Die (kid terminology) with its riding come-on. *Gentle gelding loves children, wide-open spaces, close to Hadrian's Wall.*

"I hope they have more than one gelding," Gretchen said.

"Who cares if it's a boy or girl," Wendy said. "You aren't squished in the back like those canned sardines Dad eats. If Jay would quit breathing, maybe I could see out. Riding anything is okay with me."

"I bet there's only one old nag and she probably broke her leg or died last week," Jay said. "Wash-hand basins, tea making facilities? Wow." The two younger boys kept it up. David was his usual quiet self.

"Shut up, Jay," Wendy said.

66

"Even if the place is crummy, I doubt we can cancel at this late date—no place to call out here anyway," Bev said.

The B&B was literally in a valley hole surrounded by grassy hills on the approach side, and barren moor on the other three. No River Tyne, no visible neighbors, and no horse—Biddy had died two weeks before, Mrs. Sutcliffe told the two poker-faced girls.

The only redeeming feature of Sutcliffe's was that we had the place to ourselves. The kids played hearts and checkers until bedtime. Bev and I finished off the bottle of Chablis we bought in Helmsly and, full of bangers and beans, we were on our way to climb Hadrian's Wall by 9:30 the next morning.

"What a zilch," David said. "Sorry, but broken-down rock piles don't impress me. Let's boogie." The rest of us agreed.

We managed to whip through Durham Cathedral, tombs and all, (so much for my Medieval English Art and Architecture class) and were settled on the coast near Whitby by nightfall—Captain Cook's country seemed like the height of civilization compared to the past day and a half.

Bev and I agreed—the kids deserved a commendation for good behavior in light of our final three days—too many bodies in a small space, cold, dicey weather, and a long drive home. *If you don't give it a try, how will you know whether it will work out?*

XIX ~SURPRISED BY PORTUGAL~

Dear Grandma and Grandpa,   *July 30, 1976*

I'm sorry it's taken me so long to thank you for the travel kit and clock. You can be sure it will be put to good use over the next four years. Eighteen sounds pretty old huh! My summer has been so busy I've neglected you, and Grandma and GP Jacobs, but I'll see you all soon. I'm due to arrive in Portland on the 16th of September. I can only stay a couple of days in Longview/Portland. I need to get to Eugene and pick up the stuff I've shipped before school starts.

We just got back last night (this morning) from a really great trip to Portugal. It was hot and sunny, not humid, the whole two weeks. David and I learned how to scuba dive. Now we're both qualified divers and have certificates to prove it. We only dove to around 40 or 50 feet, but it was deep enough to see lots of plant and animal life in plenty of light. The neatest part was exploring underwater caves and tunnels.

A British family I got to know had a water ski boat, so I went water-skiing quite a bit plus swimming, sun bathing, and girl-watching. I'm sure Mom will tell you all about it. Thanks again for the birthday presents. See you next month.

Love, Doug

Bev found the ad in the London Times. Two thousand dollars (1000 pounds) would get us two weeks in the Algarve (SW tip of Portugal), RT tickets for the four of us, a mini car, and a four-bedroom villa to share with the Grassmans, just 100 yards from the ocean. Since the kids had managed spring break without too many glitches, and Bev and I enjoyed each other, we decided to give it a try again. We hadn't been alone enough to really share the meat and potatoes of our lives—our ambitions, successes, sorrows, secrets. I hoped this time we would.

Bev knew Jim could be assigned to another duty at anytime. Career officers don't say no—the higher the rank, the more frequent the move. My observation was that AF families hung their pictures within days and chose friends within weeks. I wondered if moving so often was lonely for wives and hard for children. I knew I was an oddity, and I'm sure resented by some. Wes hadn't moved up the same ladder as the line officers to obtain his rank. We lived off base and I didn't go to wives' club meetings. I could do as I pleased and was happy to be free of my former (self-imposed) should's. For these three years I had the best of both worlds.

I come from a cloistered, Presbyterian, small-town-northwest background. My first 18 years were in Longview with my parents, both sets of grandparents, aunts, uncles, and cousins. Everyone thought I was a good little girl except my brother Larry (3 1/2 years my senior). Larry told me the facts of life except for those I'd gleaned from a human reproduction manual Mother gave me when I was 13. He also clued me in on more dirty words than I cared to know and their gritty meanings with the warning, "If you tell you've had it."

To my chagrin Larry saw himself as my guardian when I got to high school. When his classmate, a senior basketball star, asked me to a dance just a few months into my freshman year, of course I said yes. Larry told my parents no way. I was mortified when I had to telephone Dick Selberg and tell him I couldn't go, but I knew exactly how to get even. I hoed Erskine Caldwell's book, "God's Little Acre," out from under Larry's bed, with its grubby corners frayed from overuse, and left it on the living room coffee table.

By the time more suitable boyfriends came along, Larry was off to college. However he managed to keep his finger in that pie, so to speak, during summer and Christmas vacations. It became a serious problem after my freshman year at OSU, when I was pinned to John. When John started talking marriage I thought, *I've got a lot to do before I settle down and John isn't a candidate for happily ever after!* Unfortunately breaking up with him coincided with Larry's August wedding to my sister-in-law, Nancy. Everyone in my entire family loved John except me—*thanks so much for asking John to be an usher, Larry*— since I was maid of honor, at least I didn't have to walk down the aisle with him.

Wes and I were married the summer after we graduated. We stayed pretty close to Oregon until our England move. I had friends I'd known forever. (Except for my mother and the four years I lived in a sorority, I'd been engulfed by males my entire life.) When this trip to Portugal gelled I didn't know what I was in for. Quite frankly, I could have used Larry about then.

How would I have known that thongs weren't something one wore on one's feet, that nude beaches were the norm in Europe, that topless wasn't just in, in San Francisco bars?

Like green apples in June, you could pick us out that first day on the beach among the mostly British tourists, with our one

70

piece swim suits and the boys in boxer trunks. Problem number one occurred when a girl named Louise Phillips, on holiday with her family from Manchester for the entire month of July, spied Doug. Doug had sandy-red, wavy hair, sky-blue eyes, and a nice 18-year-old physique, plus he could lean over so far on one water ski that his elbow touched below the spray. The Phillip's ski boat was moored just off shore.

Bev's daughter Gretchen, then 16, fancied Doug, and the feeling was mutual until Louise made her parents' boat available. In short order, Doug became the talk of the beach. *Have you seen that American boy ski?* The next thing I knew Doug was giving ski lessons to the entire Phillips family while our other five kids sat in the hot sand jealously grumbling.

Bev and I decided it was time to check out the villa's very ample, shared pool— which we came to think of as our private property, since no one else was ever there. Possibly it was deserted because one had to stand on one's tip-toes and peer over a wrought-iron fence at the south end of the pool to glimpse the ocean.

Gretchen's new bathing suit was a white tank-type with red stripes. It was made of nylon and spandex (new in 1976). She was not much over five feet, with tawny soft curls pulled back in a ponytail. Gretchen had her mother's low engaging laugh and soft smile—a wholesome prettiness. No question why both Doug and David were interested. The first time she dove off the board she swam the entire length of the pool underwater. When she surfaced and stood up, Wendy yelled, "Duck, Gretchen!" The suit and liner

71

were made of a clingy fabric that showed every bump and blotch on her perfect little figure. She was humiliated.

Our villa was in Luz Bay, near a small fishing village on the outskirts of Lagos. The Luz Bay Club gift shop, frequented only by tourists like us, carried a few skimpy bikinis. Swimming suits were not big sellers in the Algarve, since every single Portuguese woman we saw was draped entirely in long black cloth and continually in mourning, we were told, for a husband, father, brother, or son. Bev had to drive 30 miles east along the coast to a larger villa development to find a suit that Gretchen would even look at.

The Luz Bay Club offered scuba diving lessons for anyone 16 or older. No way was Gretchen going to get in the club pool with Doug and David, wet suit or not. I'm sure Duncan, the boy's British expatriate instructor, knew his stuff, but he certainly didn't have the air of a professional, in his skimpy bathing trunks that fell below two ample folds of huggy-bear handles. Except for his waist rolls he was solid body and plenty of it. I saw him without his trademark wide-brimmed, floppy yellow hat covering a gray-flecked beard in the bar the day before the boy's first ocean dive. He was bald.

"Yo, Patty. Glad I ran into you. Would you and your younger boy like to join us in the Zodiac and watch your lads' trial run tomorrow?"

"We'd love to. I have a favor to ask, too," I said.

"Anything. Shoot," he said.

"Youngest son Tom is fixed on spear fishing. Would you corroborate my story? Tell him he has to be 16—no uncertain terms."

"Anytime. At your service, madam," he said with a slight bow. Whoops! I had a feeling what was coming.

"I'm through about eight," he said, raising his eyebrows. "How about coming to my place for a Pimms. Those boys of yours are fine lads. I'll detail exactly what we'll be doing and show you some pictures. There's lots of good stuff in that ocean."

"Thanks but no. I'm afraid that won't work out tonight," I said, hoping he would still take Tom and me in the boat the following day.

The Zodiac held the diving students and their gear, one English diver's wife and daughter (five or six), Tom, myself, and Duncan, who gave me a chilly wink when we climbed in. He motored about 50 yards off shore and anchored on the south side of a small bay. I didn't really notice that there were swimmers in the waters around us until Doug and David had been underwater for several minutes. One man surfaced, feet-down, face-up, within 15 feet of our boat and then dove in the opposite direction. When his bum came into view the little girl next to me said in a very loud voice, "Oouu look Mummy, he doesn't have his knickers on."

That wasn't all. I had trouble concentrating on the boys' tank lines leading into the ocean. On a cliff across from the Zodiac were at least a dozen people, bare naked (or bare mayked as Tom had called the condition since he was a toddler). They were standing up, waving to us like we were on a rescue mission. So, are nudists also exhibitionists? You got me, but I guessed many of them were British because as Wes would have said, the women were all amply endowed.

David surfaced early with an earache. He took his gear off and pretended not to notice the nudes, rather like ignoring a lit Christmas tree in the middle of the freeway. Tom kept poking me, asking if I'd seen what he saw. I was anxious for Doug, Duncan, and the other two divers to surface so we could all get out of there. This was simply a warm-up for the following day.

Before we left England, Bev and I had filled a suitcase with enough kid-food to supplement the local fare and satisfy ravenous teenage appetites—pop tarts, packaged taco mix, peanut butter, honey, kool-aid mix, hamburger helper, cheerios, etc. Bev volunteered to be head chef. Since I'd grown up at the confluence of the Columbia and Cowlitz rivers, and 50 miles from the ocean, I was fish cook.

Before breakfast every morning, Jay and David headed uphill to the village bakery, a small, round stucco house with a kiva-shaped oven built into the earth wall, to buy our daily supply of the best oval bread rolls and baguettes we'd ever eaten. Wendy and Tom usually went with Bev and me to the ocean where several fishing boats would be anchored close to the softly breaking surf. A horse drawn open wagon, wheels backed to the water's edge, was always there loading an early morning catch to deliver to Lagos. Tom and Wendy liked the fun of helping choose our dinner directly from the fishermen. The men smiled and jabbed the fish, and spoke to us in Portuguese like we could understand. Gretchen and Doug stayed home, trying not to let us notice that they were noticing each other.

At the top of the hill, a hop-skip and jump from our villa was a fruit, vegetable, and flower market with more mouth-watering choices than in the entire city of Cambridge (on occasion I have been accused of over statement). It's the only time I've eaten everything I wanted and not gained a single pound.

My guidebook described the best secluded body-surfing beach in the Algarve, near the southern most tip of Portugal—a must, it said. We piled the kids into the minis stuffed with towels and picnic food and headed south. (Thank heavens boogie boards hadn't surfaced yet). Sure enough the water looked perfect—gentle, long and rolling waves with a soft approach to the shoreline and not another soul in sight.

We hadn't finished unloading our cars when a dusty, curtained VW bus with Danish license plates pulled up and stopped within 50 feet of us. Doug, David, and Jay were heading toward the water. They turned around to look while the rest of us stood and stared at the intruders like they were from outer space. I'd seen HAIR in San Francisco, but it didn't prepare me for what came out of that bus' sliding back door.

The first guy looked like he was straight out of my old textbook, *Up From Ape,* except for his long head and facial hair— then another, whiter variety. The two began cart-wheeling like they were putting on a circus act for our enjoyment, bare naked or "mayked."

Our three older sons shot down the beach like cannon balls, missing Uma Thurman's look alike—albino-white, thin, and also bare mayked. There were a total of seven or eight unclothed hippies that emerged from that bus. Thank heavens for Gretchen and Wendy that our older boys were long gone.

Bev scuttled her girls in the other direction toward the ocean.

"It smells like they've been cooking inside their car. Something's burning," Tom said. "Why aren't they wearing bathing suits?" I decided not to say anything about staring. Impossible not to!

"There must not be laws against it here," I said, motioning him to follow Bev and the girls. "At home they could be picked up for nudity in a public place or maybe indecent exposure," I said.

"This beach isn't very public, Mom," Tom said in all his 11-year-old wisdom.

Cantaloupe was my favorite melon, unavailable during Cambridge winters. I admit to setting a very bad example for my sons when we were packing to leave. It was illegal to take fresh produce out of Portugal. When I put two cantaloupe in Tom's unlocked suitcase he balked.

"Put them in your bag. I don't want to get in trouble," he said.

"My bag has a combination lock. It's the only one they'll check. If they should find the melons, they'll just take them out of yours. Don't worry about it, and for heaven's sake don't talk about it in front of the customs agents."

Another nickname that Doug and David had given Tom was motor mouth. He has never been accused of being soft spoken. As we lined up at the bag check, Tom kept poking me and giving me dirty looks. Tom went through first and then waited next to me, breathing heavily. Sure enough they asked me to unlock my case and pawed through it, nodding when it was closed again and I was allowed to proceed. We couldn't have been more than 10 feet from the agents when Tom bellowed, "Can we talk about the cantaloupes now?"

Sometimes Tom did have foot-in-mouth disease. Fortunately for me, the agents didn't speak English.

XX ~ITALY & THE HEEL OF THE BOOT~

Wild is the way I remember the short Alitalia charter flight Tom and I took in July of 1977from Luton, England to Brindisi. Every single passenger seemed to know each other, and if they didn't I guessed they would before landing in Italy, with all that arm waving, gesturing, embracing, and rapid-fire talk. When the pilot announced the flight's descent, a hush spread over the crowd, like I imagined the quiet of the audience anticipating Churchill's announcement of D-day.

The keen silence lasted until the wheels bumped the runway and the jet came to a screeching halt. BINGO! Every single able-bodied person was clapping and yelling, "Bravo, Bravo!" *Had the pilot's ability or the plane's mechanical condition been in question, or was it simply the excitement of a homecoming?*

Wes had been sent to San Vito de Normani, a village NW of Brindisi, on the Adriatic side of Italy's heel, close to an American electronic eaves-dropping base referred to as an Antenna Farm—an espionage base that had ears reaching out in every direction, in every language imaginable.

The San Vito clinic had 'fallen below command standards.' It was in serious trouble, and had become a morale problem to personnel and their dependents. Appointments were weeks behind schedule, children weren't getting routine shots, women weren't given necessary pap smears—it was a mess. Wes had been sent there to whip the place back into shape. As a Lt. Colonel he outranked the hospital Captain, and thus could order immediate changes. The first thing he did was to cancel all leave and ordered the physicians, nurses, and other clinic personnel to work seven days a week until every appointment and test was current, and the place was functioning normally.

His popularity rating among his clinic co-workers plummeted to zero, but the rest of the military personnel on base thought of him in near-heroic terms. I was proud of him too. For his accomplishments during those two months especially, he received The Meritorious Service Medal, signed by the Secretary of the Air Force and the Commander in Chief of the United States Air Forces in Europe.

Wes had been in Italy three weeks when Tom and I arrived. He'd rented a mini-Fiat for us and reserved a motel in San Vito. I'd hoped that the three of us could spend that first weekend in Naples. We wouldn't make it this time, but something even better happened. Wes came over to the base swimming pool to find me.

"How fast can you get dressed? Doug called from the train station in Brindisi. The boys just arrived from Spain—tired, hungry, and happy to be here."

David, Doug, and Dave Bennett (Doug's best friend from Eugene) had begun their Eurail pass adventures a month earlier in

Bergen with the Milfords, through Scandinavia to Amsterdam, from Paris to the French Riviera, then to Madrid and back to Nice—and on down the leg of Italy to Brindisi.

That evening we spent over three hours in the Officers' Club dining room eating, talking, laughing, and listening while they rehashed the adventures of the past month. They consumed more steak, baked potatoes, and tossed salad than I'd ever seen them eat at home and with Tom's help, devoured an entire pie alamode sprinkled throughout with spontaneous stories.

"David tacked a sign on the Women's bathroom on a Spanish train, Roto (broken) and then went to sleep leaning against the bathroom door with his backpack," Doug laughed. "You should have seen those antsy, mad women poke him with their toes, "Idiota!"

"Give me a break!" David said. "The train was packed solid. The only space left was this rickety little area between cars with the bathrooms on either side. Dave B. and Doug glommed on to the last two empty floor spaces."

And the stories continued: about a Mafia-type Communist— "We start talking to him, then David decides to smart off, 'Viva democracia' with his fist clenched. Not smart," Doug said. "We were lucky to get off the train alive." Surely an exaggeration, I hoped, not wanting to stop their banter—another story about unrolling their sleeping bags on the beach at Biarritz. A policia told them to vamoose before they'd even crawled in. I gathered from the eye rolling, snickering, and throat-clearing that the rest of the French Riviera stories would be censored for mom-types.

For the six of us to be together before the boys' memories faded was a once in a lifetime happening. Their spontaneity was both hilarious and heartwarming. Wes and I loved every minute.

The following morning the older boys snorkeled in the Adriatic, close to the base. Dave B. caught a baby octopus and pulled it in for us to see.

"What shall I do with this guy?" Dave B. said, ready to toss it back into the ocean.

"Per favor, Signor?" a fisherman said, holding out a metal pail filled with seawater.

We'd been told that people in this part of Southern Italy were poor— violent crimes were unheard of, burglary was all too common, and car owners bought all their replacement parts on the black market. Every shop and building, including our small motel rooms (close replicas of Route 66 motels during the fifties), had bars on the windows. The mini-Fiat we rented had an inside alarm chained to the ignition key. The alarm had to be turned off before the car would start—at least rentals couldn't be hot-wired.

The four boys and I drove to a hill town (I think the name was Oria) famous for its white stucco houses with thatched, domed-roof tops that looked like giant bee hives.

One hundred lira notes (a little like Monopoly money) were illegal tender back then, but used nevertheless. Many shops had wares we'd seen in Portugal. Dave B. bought a bright multi-colored serape shirt and paid for it with several lira notes. The shopkeeper couldn't make change so he handed Dave five oranges, pointing to the rest of us. At a fruit stand on the way back to San Vito, I came away with two bananas and a telephone coin.

Three days later all six of us were swimming and picnicking on a lovely beach by the Ionian Sea. The sand was white and soft, the water clear and shallow, the sky almost cloudless. Seven or eight beautifully browned Italian children were watching our homegrown team of Dave Bennett and David Jacobs versus Doug and Tom toss a Frisbee back and forth with amazing antics—a catch three feet above Tom's head, Dave B's toss originating with a twirl from behind. The children kept edging closer and closer.

Then they divided up on either side of our American duos. The chanting, cheering, and jumping with each catch had a touch of the plane's landing excitement. Wes called to our boys, "Hold it and show their fathers your Frisbee. They're concerned." The Italian men held and looked over the Frisbee, smiled, and nodded to the children and our boys. Then they waded along the shoreline back to what I guessed were some very anxious mothers. Wes and I had spread our beach towels below a rising grassy knoll to watch them—several brown bags full of picnic food between us.

It was too shallow for snorkeling. The hot item that day was a small inflatable inner tube I'd thrown in at the last minute. Not long after her parents decided we were safe, a darling child of about six or seven sidled up to me and pointed to the tube.

"Okay Signora?" I nodded my head and smiled, "Okay." She ran with it to the water's edge, threw it out a few feet and jumped in after it, floating back and forth from her tummy to her back. After a few minutes the other kids approached her, speaking rapidly. They pointed to each other and looked up at me, then back to her. She got inside the tube, clamped her arms on either side and looked skyward.

Two girls came running up to me and began gesturing back and forth between themselves and the girl in the tube, who refused to look our way. I couldn't understand them but it was clear what they wanted.

"Take these goggles to them, Tom, "I said. "Demonstrate how to use them and then hand them to the child in the tube. Use your best sign language so she'll get the message—sharing is fun."

That kid had my number. She got out of the tube, handed the goggles to one of the older girls who had been so put out, and came lickety-split up the beach to me, this time pointing to my sack. "Signora, chocolata?"

After the three older boys left on the ferry from Brindisi to Crete, Tom and I headed south to see the cathedral and amphitheater ruins at Lecce. Finding a parking place near the cathedral was our first challenge! We secured the car—thankful to be near a busy street just two blocks from the church—so at least no one could walk away with our transportation, I thought.

The Fiat was still there when we returned to our parking spot, but unfortunately it had been squeezed into the curb with less than two feet to spare, front and back. Maneuvering out might have been manageable except for the three minis that were parked bumper to bumper on the street side of our car—we had been gone about 45 minutes. Thank heavens Tom was uninhibited!

"We can't get out of here," Tom said. "What'll we do?"

"See that policeman directing traffic on the next corner? You go get him to help. When you reach him, I'll stand here and wave."

"What if he doesn't speak English?" Tom said.

"Use your best sign-language. I'll do the same from the street here." Within five minutes, Tom had the policeman and two other smiling Italians ready to assist. The three men literally picked up the Fiat and lifted it over the cars into the open street.

"Grazie, grazie, grazie," Tom called out the window as we drove away.

On the way back to the base we stopped to see a section of The Appian Way, a cobbled Roman highway over 2200 years old that still runs all the way from Rome to Brindisi.

"I guess Romans worked more in Italy than at Hadrian's Wall," Tom said. "This old road looks a lot better kept than the ruins and stuff in England."

Christmas at Ivy House

St. Anton, Austria

Lunch in Liechtenstein

With Crists and Walkers at Linderhof Castle

The Matterhorn, Switzerland

Zermatt, Switzerland

Patty and Doug at Hitler's Eagles Nest

Entrance to Dachau
"WORK TO BE FREE"

XXI EUSTON HALL & NADFAS

Say you're sitting next to me and a dozen other late 40 and 50-year-old women around a mid-July campfire. The light has faded to the color of hemlock bark. We can hear the busy Rogue rushing and tossing nearby and pull up the hoods on our sweatshirts. Our three Ouzel Outfitter guides have locked and bear-weighted the coolers and stored them under one of the over-turned rafts.

We've been comparing camp and college songs we learned as kids, feeling happily tired and mellow after an exciting day on the water and a second glass of wine.

"You gals ever play two truths and a lie?" Peter said. "Great loosen-upper."

"It goes like this," he said. "I ask Patty to tell me two truths about herself and one lie. My example—I sang tenor with the New York Philharmonic. I've guided over 100 parties down the Rogue. I got a business degree from the U of O in 1984. So which one's the lie?" he said. We chime in—*you can't carry a tune. Singing tenor. Yeah!*

"You really know how to hurt a guy! Okay Patty, you're first."

"This is hard," I said, looking at my friend Zilpha. "She's known me since junior high. Okay. I played viola at Kessler Junior High School. At our final concert we stood up on stage to bow. The safety pin in my mother's garter belt popped open and my stockings fell down around my ankles."

"I'll never tell!" Zilpha said with a straight face.

"I was a stately home guide at Euston Hall in Suffolk, England. And, lets see. I saw what Harry Truman swore was Big Foot's print on the shore at Spirit Lake, before Mt. St. Helens erupted."

You guess while I turn back in time to England.

Edward Joy might have been titled honorary member emeritus of the Newmarket Decorative and Fine Arts Society (NADFAS). He was definitely the persona grandee in the group. Silvia Horwood-Smart, a woman outwardly as lofty as her name, was chairman. She was a small woman with an Oxford, Karo-syrup accent and shrill voice that increased in volume when she wished to be heard. Besides that, someone in Mrs. Horwood-Smart's family was distantly related to the Queen! She told me she was extremely fond of Emily and Edward Joy the day she invited me to lunch with them at her home "preceding our visit to Euston Hall." I was nervous.

The Joys had invited me to be their monthly guest at NADFAS, held in Newmarket's Assembly Hall with lectures given by authorities in the various arms of English Arts. You couldn't really say arts and crafts, at least in relationship to the lectures I heard. For example, English porcelain collectors' pieces (pronounced exactly as spelled, poor-ce-lain) often dated back two hundred years and were very elaborate. They wouldn't be at home in my house! By comparison, contemporary German Hummel figurines looked like child's clay-play.

On the NADFAS monthly meeting days close to a hundred people gathered in the hall. Even if I hadn't been personally introduced to them, I could invariably pick out the titled women in their hats and fur neck pieces. As the youngest person there, with an American accent and a comfort zone of zero, I'm afraid I stood out like a sore thumb. I was happiest during the lights-out slide presentations. I could do my deep breathing, relaxation exercises unnoticed, with Emily dozing at my side.

The lunch at Sylvia's (*please do call me Sylvia)* began with a glass of sherry in the drawing room at 11:30a.m. The fire was lit in a large fireplace with what Edward described as a Gibbons style chimney-piece (an elaborate carved wood sconce surrounding a mirror hung over the matching wood mantle). Boy would my mother disapprove of this scene—drinking anytime was verboten, even a civilized sherry. Sherry before lunch—no way!

Lunch was served in the formal dining room. Starter, entrée, dessert— back home in lumber town Longview, we're talking main holiday meal. The soup was creamed asparagus. The entrée, roast beef and Yorkshire pudding, the dessert, a lemon custard (the pudding). Sylvia apologized for skipping the cheese and cracker course to "brave the storm and be prompt for our 2:30 p.m. appointment" at Euston Hall, the Duke and Duchess of Grafton's stately home in Suffolk.

Because Edward was leading our party, the Duke asked if we would like to tour their private quarters upstairs. I decided to make the most of this opportunity and dogged right along on Edward's heels as he pointed out the discrepancies in furniture styles. As I remember the Duke's bedroom was furnished ala Dutch (bed, tables, dressers), distinguishable by thick heavy wooden legs and bulbous feet—very masculine-looking.

As a NADFAS member, I naively volunteered to be a guide at Euston Hall one Thursday a month during the summer. With my official badge in place, I sat near the door of the library ante-room on a very uncomfortable Chippendale chair, hoping the paying visitors wouldn't ask any questions I couldn't answer. I had plenty of time to think.

Did these elaborately decorated rooms get full of elegant furnishings and famous paintings at the expense of my puritan ancestors? Would my fascination with England continue if I lived here indefinitely? By sitting here pretending I belong, am I in a small way reinforcing a life style that I wouldn't want to be part of?

It was all so new, fun, and frivolous then, but now when Wes teases me about England and says I should have lived two hundred years ago, a lady-in-waiting to the Queen, I tell myself no way. I belong near the woods and water—fishing or floating on the Rogue, kayaking on a coastal lake, searching for sand dollars and snowy plovers at the Siltcoos Inlet. The Pacific Northwest is in my blood. It's always been home.

So, the lie would have been Big Foot's print. With apes living in the woods under Spirit Lake (before the eruption, that is), Big Foot would have avoided the place like the plague.

Dear Mother and Dad,   *November 15, 1976*

Your Christmas packages arrived already! I'll mail yours next week. Then I plan to relax between Thanksgiving and the holidays. The English stay inside more during these short, cold, windy days. I'm not sure what they're doing, but I have a feeling it's not the merry-go-round of bake-off, buying, and party planning that many Americans seem to be caught up in this time of year. My New Year's Resolution will be: Kick the holiday "shoulds" good-by forever. Think I'll make it?

Netta Kennedy and I went to London yesterday to do some shopping and saw the matinee, "No Sex Please, I'm British." It was terribly funny, plus we had a tongue-in-cheek laugh during intermission! We went to the Swiss Center before the play to buy some cheese. Netta was making raclette, a cheese melt dish with boiled potatoes, dill pickles, and little white onions, to serve some vegetarian guests that weekend. She slipped her bag containing the cheese on the floor between our seats. Unfortunately there was a heat vent there as well—well, we spent the first half sniffing, laughing, then looking at each other, then the people around us to see who'd had bangers and beans for lunch! During intermission she got rid of the raclette while I sat red-faced, imagining everyone within earshot was looking at me disdainfully...

You know how we light up our houses? Not here! No one has lights outside in Stetchworth. In fact all winter after 5:00 p.m. they close all the shades and doors and heat only the kitchen and television room. Electricity is a treasured commodity. So I issued the boys a lights-off ultimatum after arriving home from London to a dark village except for Ivy House, which looked like a giant advertisement for General Electric. They're complying. None of us want to be labeled ugly Americans.

If asked to pick a favorite time of year at Ivy House, I think I would have to choose Christmas. It was pitch dark by 4 p.m. in

December, there was often a biting wind off the North Sea, and our packages to the States had long since been mailed.

The half-timbered fireplace mantles looked perfect with the fresh pine and cedar-scented boughs we'd gathered draped over them. None of the shops and stores in Newmarket or Cambridge were strewn with the glitz and glitter so familiar back home, and the streets with an occasional sprinkling of snow had a quiet, soft-velvet feeling. Everyone settled down indoors.

We invited the Lehrs for Christmas dinner—Doreen, Wayne, their daughter Deborah, and Doreen's mother from Devon. I decided to go all-out English, at least as much as I'd picked up about their customs from TV, reading Dickens, or watching the Nutcracker. I bought Christmas crackers, those gold, silver, red, and green-papered favors with black powder-coated pulls at each end. When jerked simultaneously with a partner the crackers bang loudly and pop open, exposing novelty fillings of jokes, fortunes, small trinkets like dice, a ring, or jacks, and most importantly, a paper crown.

After 28 years of continuing this Christmas cracker tradition in our family, the paper crown is still the biggy. Only the secure, fun-loving person will wear these tissue crowns throughout dessert, confident that the head-piece doesn't make one look silly. Doug was told this fact throughout his late teens and early 20s, every time he'd set the hat aside or put it on for a max of three minutes.

Of course Doreen's family had grown up with crackers—so picture the two hat-ted families seated around a rectangular, candle lit table between dinner and dessert, reading the jokes and fortunes out loud, waiting for the Christmas pudding. I'd lined fresh holly around the pudding, centered it on a silver tray and told Wes to pour a half cup of 150 proof rum over the top (he said the pudding looked suspiciously like my mother's fruitcake only heavier) and light it. Whoom! Thank heavens the poppers on the crackers were spent because the holly caught on fire—we're talking near catastrophe!

"Whooooo," Wes said, turning on his heel like he'd just heard a starter gun pop—out to the kitchen sink to wet down the sputtering, fortunately slightly-green holly and alcohol-singed cake.

"I've had a lot of Christmas puddings," Doreen's mother said, "But I've never had one quite like this before."

After the fire was doused, and over the pumpkin and mincemeat pies I'd made just in case, I learned that the pudding should have been steamed in a double boiler for at least an hour. Obviously I chucked the Christmas pudding and the tradition before it was established. No question though, I'll hear about it every Christmas until my dying day.

"They're going to be exhausted," Wes said on his way out the door to work. "Don't over-program. London's the day after tomorrow."

"Yes Sir," I said out loud, saluting the closed door.

Monday was a bank holiday. Tom and I were on our way to Heathrow to pick up our Eugene friends Martie and Bob Crist and Jean and Doug Walker who would be with us off and on for three weeks—the second week the six of us would spend on the continent in a rented VW bus.

Tom was as excited to see them as I was. Our young families had grown up together, traded babysitting, skied at Mt. Bachelor and Hoodoo together— tail-gated in the snow. Having Steve Crist and Tom Walker's parents' come to visit was the next best thing to seeing his friends.

"Who gets to sleep in my bunk beds?" Tom asked.

"I think we'll have them flip for it," I said.

"Are you going to tell them about the ghost in the guest room?" he said.

"I'll leave that up to you."

Our passengers were in tow by two o'clock, we'd cleared northwest London and were heading toward Cambridge. I decided to swing by Ely Cathedral, 20 minutes from home. If the four of them could avoid napping, have a very early dinner, and get right to bed, it might ease their jet lag the following day.

Eleventh-century Ely Cathedral rose dramatically above the flat, fenland countryside about five miles ahead.

"Wake up! Ivy House on the horizon," I said.

"Wow. Nice digs. No wonder you like living here," Bob said, leaning away from the right door. "Those people driving on the wrong side of the road are giving me the willies—heading right for me. No way I'll close my eyes."

"We'll come back and look inside the cathedral when you've had some sleep. It's magnificent," I said, driving around the west entrance. "Oliver Cromwell lived here for several years during the Reformation—he did a lot of damage inside, especially in the Lady Chapel." I'd stopped in front of the half-timbered Steward's House called Cromwell House.

"Refresh me on the Reformation," Jean said.

"All good Catholics should know about Cromwell's puritan stint as England's protectorate," Bob said. "He shattered Ireland's military forces and smashed churches to smithereens, then came here and did another bang up job."

All of us were personal friends of Sister Monica Heeran, the CEO of Sacred Heart Hospital in Eugene. Tom pointed to Cromwell house and said, "When Sr. Monica was visiting, she asked Mom to take her picture right there. She said her mother would roll over in her grave if she could see her then, and guess what?"

"What?" a chorus of four.

"Sister had the film developed while she was staying with us, and that was the only picture that didn't turn out."

Bob and Doug were runners. Bob claimed the best thing about running was the calories you burn up—'then you can eat anything you want.' Bob had gone out alone the next morning. The Duke's game warden hailed him down to tell him he was on private property. By the time he got back to relay the story it was typical, un-intimidated Bob!

"Nice guy. He showed me Milreef, a beautiful horse we can buy for a measly 5000 pounds."

"I better go with you next time," Doug said. "I don want to bail you out of jail, or worse yet, the poor house."

We had tickets for *Chorus Line* on Wednesday night. After that the Crists and Walkers would spend several days in London while Wes and I headed home. When I picked the foursome up in Cambridge two days later they were brimming with excitement and talk of London's treasures. They had raved about the musical too— an exaggeration! Martie was the only one that hadn't nodded off— *had I planned too much too soon?*

I was happy to pass the baton to Wes. At the base he'd purchased the flight and train tickets, enough 'funny money' for our group, and reserved a Volkswagen bus, roomy enough for six of us, our luggage, and the picnic supplies we'd pick up in Switzerland. Suzie, the same corpsman that stayed with the kids before, was very contentious. This time she insisted on bringing her own wheels, promised to keep a close eye on the cat and enjoy the boys. I could relax.

It was Martie's birthday and a group decision (I emphasize group because I can't believe I did what I did). In Geneva while the men picked up the bus, Jean kept Martie busy watching suitcases and reading maps. I slithered over to the magazine kiosk. I thought I'd lucked out. No one was at the counter except a grandmotherly looking clerk with half glasses, frowning at me as I thumbed through the magazine rack, trying to be nonchalant. I found *Playboy,* but where the heck was *Playgirl,* if there even was such a magazine. (*Was this joke on Martie or me?*).

Then the worst! I found a copy of *Playgirl,* turned it over with the back cover up and fished into my Swiss change purse. A slick- looking Asian guy in Gucci shoes (I know because the floor was the only place I would have dared look at that point) appeared from nowhere, stood almost shoulder to shoulder and said, "You like magazine, yes?" I handed Brunhilda (I think she was the one that let out that snort) the magazine and a bill I hoped would cover the cost, turned on my heels and almost ran, wishing I were a genie that could slide back in a bottle or anything else that would take me somewhere besides there! Tokyo Tim was following me, "Hey wait! Where you stay?"

On our first picture stop by Lake Geneva in Montreux, I told Martie, "I'll never forget your thirty-ninth birthday. If you weren't such a good friend, I'd consider jumping in the lake with your racy present and never surfacing."

"For some strange reason, it's missing. Help me find it and we'll both have a good laugh," she said.

The drive up a winding, narrow road to Vissoie, a small French-speaking village— up, up beside a deep precipice with few guardrails, was exciting, scary, and gorgeous all at once, if one had the courage to look down and back. The three rooms we found at the Pension de la Poste were just 23 Swiss Francs per person a night including breakfast ($20 a couple), and it was perfect. Very black coffee, fabulous Swiss cheese and fresh bread. 'Merci, merci,' for this perfect night and morning—down pillows and comforters that smelled like the crisp, clear air outside, window boxes thick with bright red geraniums and cascading white petunias, eight church bells tolling time for breakfast that morning, and friends to share it with.

Jean is responsible for the particulars I've written about this week-long trip. She's always has had an eye for detail—so obvious in the great journal she kept from years ago, with illustrations, no less.

Wes was the photographer on that awesome trip across the Swiss and Austrian Alps in October sunshine—their snowcaps crowned with cotton-candy clouds against a sapphire blue sky. I wonder how we could have been so lucky. Up the steep Grimsell Pass and around every turn the oohs and ahs continued, then down into the swishy town of Interlaken to buy picnic food and laugh about hob-nobbing with the rich and famous.

From the decking around the three bedroom Gasthaus we found at Grindelwald, you could see the Eiger and Jungfrau towering above the chalets that dotted the green meadows below their snow capped peaks. We wouldn't have seen people sweeping and washing walks and walls, or heard the chorus of tinkling cowbells, in Mt. Rainer National Park, but somehow all the flowers and sloping hills that surrounded the base of those mountains reminded me of places back home.

We went through sprawling Davos before any snow had fallen, on the first gray day since Geneva. For whatever reason, and after all I'd read about that health spa/resort town, Davos was disappointing. Susch, Switzerland (through the Fluela Pass about 30 miles from Austria) was another story. A tiny village with an onion domed church, a castle ruins, and the pretty Steinbock Hotel all to ourselves for $24 per couple, breakfast included—"good enough for the girls I go with," Doug said after checking out their room.

After the Austrian Alps, our last stop was the commissary in Garmisch, Germany to buy gas and load up on enough drinks, lunch, and hors d'oeuvre food to last us through the train trip to Paris. We'd just finished loading the car and Wes had the key in the ignition when two plain clothes, Dragnet-looking guys knocked on the driver's side window. Elliot Ness flashed his badge, nodded, and asked Wes to step out of the bus. Through the rolled down windows, Elliot's partner looked each one of us over, eyeball to eyeball.

We hadn't done anything illegal, immoral, or even distasteful (minus Martie's long-gone, R-rated magazine, gulp). We weren't talking box-loads of supplies, and this may sound defensive, but I can't think of three more square-ish, preppy-looking couples among the people I know.

The men were OSI (Officers of Special Investigations, the military's F.B. I.). After Wes showed them his Air Force I.D. and leave papers, and told them we were vacationing with friends from Oregon, and that we'd picked up the Volkswagen in Geneva and were returning it to Zurich, they relaxed and nodded.

"It was the bus with Swiss license plates," Wes said, obviously shaken. "They'd never seen the combination on this base before. Just checking to be sure we had the right to be shopping in an American commissary."

After returning the Volkswagen to Zurich, taking the train to Basel, and boarding our Paris-bound train we settled into our first class compartment (well done Wes) and began thinking about lunch. This was the Orient Express route of old that started in Istanbul and ended in London.

I have no recollection of breakfast that morning, and certainly none of us had any reservations about busying ourselves with lunch preparations. Tray tables were out. Jean was slicing Swiss cheese, Doug was spreading deviled ham from a tin onto crackers, Bob was opening a bottle of white German wine, and I was fishing in the basket for dill pickles when the porter came in to take our luncheon order.

"Par 'don, if you please," he said. Then, looking from one tray table to another in disbelief, he took a deep breath—"Excuse me!" and left.

We knew before we left Stetchworth that our Paris arrival coincided with a fashion convention and hotels were booked solid. My Fielding Guide for traveling in Europe with children saved the day. *Hotel d'Athenis, inexpensive/near Opera house/ ninety-six F. per night with shower.* We'd been spoiled in Switzerland and Germany. Our Paris bedroom was small with tall French windows that faced an alley. The floor slanted, the shower dribbled, and the toilet in the hall was, let's say, funny.

Since Wes and I were leaving for home the next day it didn't matter to us—Crists and Walkers were staying on, and as usual were great sports! They reported later it was just fine. "All we need is a place to sleep in a city like Paris," Martie said.

It was a clear autumn late afternoon and evening. Wes and I walked and walked past Left Bank shops and sidewalk cafes and then met the others at a small restaurant recommended by Eugeneans, La Petit Panone. When it came to ordering I should have shut up. I'd taken a five-day French cooking class in Dieppe the previous May, and must have needed to tell about my newly acquired skill. Gracious, unassuming Martie, with her amazing recall of college French (a Phi Beta Kappa) was, as usual, thoughtfully quiet—with the men in this group I was asking for trouble.

Jean and Doug ordered bouillabaisse and crudités (at least I was right about green salad). Their soup arrived in a huge pot with two small flat fish floating on top—yuk! I ordered crustace, expecting small crayfish or crab. What arrived was a long, skinny, lobster-looking shellfish, upside down in a glass bowl with pinchers reaching for my chin. Period. In spite of a tiny fork and nut-cracker type instrument, I had no idea how to proceed, or remember whether I managed to extract any meat from the body of that thing.

"What kind of a class did you say you'd taken?" Doug said.

Two bottles of wine between the six of us and we were ready for dessert! The others probably had something safe like crème caramel. I knew what I wanted—Le pomme! I expected a lovely round apple dessert, possibly dipped in caramel, oozing with sugar. What came was a single green apple on a small plate with a knife to cut.

Martie and Jean didn't say a word. But Bob and Doug let me have it.

"So you speak Francais? Took a week-long cooking school? Know all the ropes? Too bad you're going home. Can't imagine how we'll fare without you."

David's 16th birthday was on January 22, 1976. We took the boys out of school for a family ski trip to St. Anton, Austria, a charming snow covered village nestled at the base of the Austrian Alps. Facing east down the street from our hotel, the St. Antoner Hof, was a lovely small onion-domed church. The shops and pensions lining the village were creamy-white with brown wooden overhangs, windows, and window boxes—none over four stories high. The pastry shop was half way between the hotel and the church. Every day after skiing the boys stopped at the bakery for "the greatest chocolate éclairs" to tide them over until supper. Then all five of us eagerly ate dinner and collapsed until the following morning. Skiing St. Anton was rigorous!

Before Wes left with the guide he'd hired as David's birthday gift he warned me, "Leave your Mrs. polite, everyone-gets-their-turn hat at home when you and Tom get in that lift line. Germans don't cue like the British. It's guts ball out there! Let Tom take the lead and just keep up with him. No eye contact or you'll get hammered." It didn't take long to see what he meant. I could almost feel hot cocoa breath through my parka, the backs of my skis were stepped on a least a dozen times, and I could have grabbed the person's pole behind me if I'd wanted to pick a fight.

With the guide, Wes, David and Doug were the first foursome up the lift on a newly opened mountain trail. David said they had at least nine runs on fresh, un-skied powder—the most perfect snow he'd ever skied. 'My birthday was so neat,' he wrote my parents. 'I got the Olympic commemorative coins for 1976, and the people at our hotel baked me a special cake. There's this great mural about eight feet long, like a huge photo along the stairs in our hotel, a panorama of the Austrian Alps, naming all the mountains and ski areas...'

I ordered two more-than-ample fondues, a beef and a cheese for David's birthday dinner. Even the boys had to stop before the pots were empty to save room for dessert. The chef suggested his specialty, a meringue pudding/cake with frothy white, oval mounds piled in a cone shape on top of one another. Some might describe the chef's melt-in -your mouth *Magic Mountain* as decadent. But somehow, leaving any part of it seemed like a cardinal sin.

To say our family ski trip to Switzerland the following year was anything less than marvelous would be an injustice. The skiing at Zermatt surpassed any I remember—going all the way back to my pre-teen years as a beginner at Mt. St. Helens and Mt. Hood. The snow had a nice pack with just a hint of powder. The runs were all perfectly groomed. Wes and the older boys loved skiing the deep powder and steep uncharted runs at St. Anton. I was a fair-weather skier. It helped that the sun was out the entire week.

Hi Grandma and Grandpa,

The picture is of the Matterhorn, 6,094 meters high— awesome! To the right of the mountain is Italy. Today we took a lift up to the Italian-Swiss border with a guide. Tom went back and forth across the borderline 50 times, so now he can say he was in Italy and

Switzerland 50 times on Monday, January 31ˢᵗ. Then we skied down the mountain to Cervinia, Italy, and had pizza for lunch. There was only one yukky bathroom for everybody at the restaurant and it had a flowery-glazed window in the door. Mom said you couldn't see through but she's wrong. Switzerland is beautiful and really clean...
Love, David

Zermatt was larger than St. Anton but every bit as charming. Horse-drawn carriages taxied people down narrow lanes, there were many more chalets and hotels— even a large ice skating rink. To say the week flew by is putting it mildly.

Tom and I shared what I'd call a spiritually carnal experience on our last day in Zermatt. Wes and the older boys had taken a cross-country trail that half-circled the Matterhorn on the previous day and raved about how beautiful it was. Since we were slower, Tom and I usually skied the easier, well-packed runs.

"You won't want to miss this chance," Wes said. "It's flat, easy cross country and the scenery is unbelievable."

Tom and I got off the lift where the trail started. Four or five skiers, maybe 400 yards ahead of us, rounded a bend and were out of sight. We were completely alone with the sun at our backs moving like silent pilgrims, gazing skyward at the Matterhorn with its sharp hooked peak reaching toward a cloudless heaven. The sunny side of the mountain glistened white, then onyx-dark on its stone outcroppings and jagged precipices.

"Take some pictures," Tom said in a whisper.

The camera was back at our hotel. *What a way to go*, I told myself over and over about this day, my very last day of skiing.

XXV ~MUNICH & DACHAU

If Berlin was the capital of Hitler's world, the Eagle's Nest was his private sentinel, perched at the top of the Bavarian Alps. On a September day straight from central casting, Doug, Wes, and I stood on that mountain top awed and somewhat overwhelmed as we looked out over what seemed like a million mountain peaks stretching in every direction, cloud banks covering valleys—majestic and surreal. We hadn't yet been tainted by our visit to Dachau.

After a year majoring in forestry at OSU (all three terms on the Dean's List), Doug decided he wasn't sure about spending his life in the woods. The travel bug had bitten. His bent for languages, the close proximity to England, and the possibility that we'd be returning to the U.S. in a year gave credence to him spending his sophomore year at the University of Maryland's Munich branch.

It hadn't really registered on me that Munich was the former Nazi party headquarters, and Bavaria the playground of that horrible mastermind Hitler, who with his henchmen killed a third of the world's Jewish population. We'd still have given our consent, but I certainly would have boned up big time on my history lessons.

Doug had had all of two months in Munich when Wes and I ferried to Belgium, drove to Bavaria, and stayed at a pension close to the campus to see him. His halting German worked perfectly on the Strassenbahn, a three-car electric-powered tram that took us right into the heart of old Munich—all quaint, cobble stoned, and squeaky clean.

"You're gonna love Malteaser's," Doug said, and it was a fun place, although ouch! Tripping on the entry steps and falling to my knees with my hands splayed out in front of me was extremely embarrassing—this before being served one of the world's largest steins of beer! Doug and Wes were very kind, blaming my new one-inch-heel leather boots and a poor night's sleep. But it wasn't the first time I'd taken a spill and as before, it was very worrisome.

Malteaser's beer garden was in a storied building with a restaurant at the top. After dinner we followed the oomph-pa-pa music downstairs to a large auditorium-like room on the ground floor filled with tables of swigging, singing Germans. On a small elevated stage, a band of men dressed in lederhosen held up with colorful suspenders were playing accordion, tuba, rinki-tink piano, horn, and fiddle to a rousing bandleader's beat.

An elderly man at a front table (gray hair and pot belly were give-aways) stood up and began singing, and slopping some of his stein in the process—no microphone necessary! The bandleader jumped off the stage, replaced the man's mug with his baton, and to our complete amazement ushered him carefully up the steps. Guiding the fellow's baton arm, the bandleader let him direct a short piece, motioned the audience to clap, thanked him profusely, and carefully shuttled him back to his seat.

"I've seen this happen before," Doug said. "The Germans have so much respect for their elders, and are so kind to them. At home we'd be embarrassed and usher a drunk to the door. You'd never see that happen here!"

Doug believed all Germans had an inside track on the treatment of elderly people, and that Americans including his parents, could learn a few things from them.

The following day when we saw the stark hole through cement, the prisoners' entrance to Dachau with the sign *WORK WILL MAKE YOU FREE,* and realized that farms and the neighboring village of Dachau were just 10 miles northwest of Munich, Doug's assumptions would have been impossible for anyone to believe—impossible not to have heard gun shots, impossible not to have seen starving prisoners through barbed wire, impossible not to smell the horrid stench from the crematorium.

As a result of Germany's unconditional surrender agreement with the Allies after WWII, their concentration and death camps were to be maintained and open to the public. The two story guard towers, the heavy, high, barbed-wire fencing, and the small museum that included pictures of prisoners who had been incarcerated and died right there—that's where the tour began, where I felt like I had lived and died with them as well. I was literally throwing-up sick before we even approached the yard and grounds. Without speaking it became clear to all three of us that this wasn't an aberration of a small number of Germans. It was hell on earth.

We saw a barracks building that reminded me of a large human chicken-coop with single bunk boards three prisoners deep and four tiers high—sleeping up to sixteen people. We saw the shower chamber where naked people expecting to be washed clean were gassed, and the ovens where human bodies were cremated.

When we finally spoke, I don't remember what we said, but maybe we expressed hope to one another that this permanent display of the horrid, savage, and brutal treatment at Dachau and other German death camps—when human beings had been murderously, tortuously inhuman would insure that this type of thing would never, ever happen again.

XXVI ~MY DIAGNOSIS ~

Dear Mother and Dad,   *November 1, 1978*

 I've just mailed a tape that I hope will arrive soon after this letter. It will give you details from the C.A.T. scan and tests I had in Cambridge. I thought it would be easier than talking by phone. The news isn't as bad as it might have been. My neurologist says forty-two is old for MS. If the diagnosis is correct, I shouldn't be too disabled.

 I guess what I want to ask of you and other family and friends is to treat me like you always have. I plan to carry on with life and do as much as I can after I see what my limitations are. I hope you'll feel comfortable telling your friends if I do have MS—after all it can't be helped and isn't shameful.

 You know how I love to read and my eyes are just fine! I'm still the very same person I always have been—a very very fortunate daughter, wife, and mother.
With love always,
Patty

These chapters began with me waking from a dream where Mother was foremost in my mind. She had told me more than once, "No matter what happens to you in your life you'll be able to handle it." Mother believed and lived the *golden rule*—with special attention to those less fortunate. I've tried to replicate and remember her example.

 She loved to be outdoors. We camped and hiked, picked huckleberries, dug razor clams side by side, ran from a black bear on a switch back above Spirit Lake, and laughed about it later. I think of her every single day with love and thanks. If I showed naïve bravery in the late seventies and early eighties, I credit her. I needed her endowment of courage then, every speck of it, to face what happened during those last six months in England and after our trip to Germany to see Doug.

David and Tom were back in school that sunny morning when my friend Ruth and I met at the Mildenhall Base to play several sets of singles. I must have served first and we volleyed. I don't remember that part. Then I tried to run to the net for a short ball but my legs simply wouldn't move. I wasn't tired or winded—nothing hurt. I remember distinctly a weird, weak feeling, and a tingling sensation that began at the top of my head and flashed down my spine like a tiny charge of electricity.

"Are you okay?" Ruth asked.

"Something's wrong. My legs won't go," I said, taking short, stiff baby steps toward the net. Nothing like this had ever happened to me before. My head felt like it held a dozen cat eyes glowing in the dark.

"Do you want me to drive you home? Someone can pick up your car later," Ruth said, sounding as scared as I was feeling. One at a time I tried to bend my legs and knees and alternately shake them. My left leg wasn't working right and felt tingly. I stood up, took several deep breaths, and told myself *pull yourself together.* When I walked slowly off the court, the flashing, numbing sensation temporarily disappeared.

"I'll be okay," I told Ruth. "I'll take it easy going home and call you when I get there."

By the time Wes came home for dinner I seemed okay, but was still scared spit less. I told him what happened. He asked me how I'd slept the previous night, and jokingly asked whether I'd had too many glasses of wine—I wish! After dinner that night, or maybe it was the following night we went for a walk through the village and up a slight incline to Devil's Dike (built during Roman times) that skirted the Duke's property. Wes was walking behind me when I caught my left foot on a tree root in the trail and almost fell. Then I caught it a second time and reached for his arm. I had to lift my left leg and swing it a bit to move forward.

"Stop a minute, honey. Your left foot's dragging. Okay, walk ahead again. Does your heel or ankle hurt?" He sounded very worried.

"Nothing hurts. My leg isn't working right is it?" I felt that just-about-ready-to cry feeling welling up in my chest and throat.

"No. Your left foot is dropping. Let's head home the way we came, it's shorter," he said. "I'm going to call Ray tonight. We'll get you into the base to see him first thing in the morning."

Major Ray Englander was a young neurologist from New York with a citified, sophisticated background (his parents were both classical musicians) that didn't show up at first glance. After his residency he was assigned to Lakenheath. His office was next door to Wes'. Ray had (I should say has) freckles, rusty-wavy hair, and a cute Mickey Rooney smile. His cuddle factor hadn't gone unnoticed by the single women on the base.

"What's going on with you?" he said. His voice was calming. I repeated what I'd told Wes the night before and mentioned that after a hot shower I'd had trouble walking down the long hall to our bedroom without hanging onto the wall.

"Let's talk a bit more. I'm going to do a few preliminary tests on you, and then we'll schedule you in this week. This may take several days."

Ray was patient, kind, and methodical as he guided me through every neurological test available at Lakenheath in 1978. I'm thankful he was the first doctor I saw (he's still my neurologist in Eugene).

A technologist attached wires to my head while I gazed at a flashing black and white checkerboard screen. Ray looked in my eyes with an ophthalmoscope--clicking lenses and flashing lights till I felt like my head must be a translucent ball. He hammered on my knees, ankles, and wrists. I followed his pointing finger with my eyes, back and forth, up and down. He watched me walk—toe to heel, heel to toe, try to hop (neither worked). I tried to squat and couldn't get back up.

"This is really bad," I said to Ray, wishing I could run and hide somewhere and cry my eyes out. I was sick of everyone (technicians, nurses, friends) telling me how brave I was being when really I felt like I did as a child, anticipating a penicillin shot in my hip. *It will hurt! I'll never walk again. What if I fall and my legs are too weak to pick myself up?*

"Before we talk about your test results I'd like to have Wes with us," Ray said after several days of appointments. Wes was waiting outside the door. We sat across the desk from Ray.

"I've done every test available here. I'm sending you to see Dr. Yealland at Addenbrooks in Cambridge. He's the department head of neurology, an outstanding physician. He'll be doing a brand new procedure on you, a C.A.T. scan. The scanner will take pictures of your spine and brain. He'll do other tests too, some of the same ones I've done. Addenbrooks is a teaching hospital, so there'll be student participation. The same things we've done will be repeated, and it'll take several days. Are you okay with that?"

"Yes," I said softly, trying to suppress the tears that lay waiting every time I opened my mouth.

Student participation—question after question after question: "Did you have pets in your childhood home?" "Yes. Cocker Spaniel's. I used to kiss Rusty right on his mouth and he'd lick me back." "Did you have a childhood illness that confined you to bed?" "Yes. When I was in third grade I had strep throat. I was in bed for six weeks. Dr. Pulliam came to our house every week to give me a penicillin shot in my hip." "Have you always lived in the Northern Hemisphere?" "Yes, except for 18 months in Port Hueneme, California, when I was twenty-eight." "Can you pinpoint the onset other than when you were playing tennis?" "Several times before that, when I felt very tired and put upon, or was emotionally upset, I'd feel a zinging flash, like an electric shock that started at the top of my head and went down my spine." "What kinds of things upset you?" "I'd rather not say."

"All the tests we've given you the past few days lead to one of two possibilities. Many symptoms point to Multiple Sclerosis. The leg drop, tingling and numbness, incontinence, sensitivity to heat, and fatigue," Ray said. "Nothing shows in your upper body. Your eyes aren't affected—partial blindness is often the case with MS patients, so that's good. The other possibility is a spinal tumor."

"What do you think it is?" I asked. Wes handed me his hanky and took hold of my hand.

"I wish I knew, Patty. You're fortunate to be in the right place at the right time. This new C.A.T. scanner should give us some answers. We'll decide how to proceed from there," Ray said.

Self-pity hovered over me like the cream-soup fog outside that November afternoon as I lay on the sofa, watching the window for Tom's school bus. Emily had stopped in with a potted yellow freesia plant that reminded me of spring, and made me wonder about my new wait-and-see how it progresses disease. The C.A.T. scan ruled out a spinal tumor. *It's not cancer. At least I'm going to live.*

Ray had explained the two common forms MS took: exacerbating and remitting, which usually occurred between the ages of 20 and 40, and chronic progressive (now called primary progressive) a slower, less severe type, more common in people my age.

For the next five months I teeter-tottered between denial and anger, trying to pretend all was well, at least in public. The facts were; a slow fourth of a mile on flat ground was about as far as I could walk, lukewarm water was all I could tolerate, I was tired all the time. Wes was more realistic. He cancelled our plan to take one last ski trip to the French Alps.

"Don't worry about disappointing the boys," he said, rubbing his lips over the back of my hand. "We can ski all we want in Oregon." *He can. The boys will. I mightn't be able to even walk cross-country.* I thought about climbing to the very top of Mt. St. Helens with my brother Larry and writing "Hi Mom" in the crusty August snow. I thought about my summer as hike master at the Longview Y.M.C.A. Camp, Spirit Lake, when I was twenty. I thought about our family back packing in the Three Sisters Wilderness and swimming in an icy glacial lake. If someone so much as snapped their fingers—right then and there, I'd have burst into tears.

My anger would kick in big time when we returned home, as I jealously watched trails crowded with joggers along the Willamette River. When reality settled in I would grieve over my inability to participate in so many outdoor activities that had been a part of my former self. It took several years until I adjusted to a new way of life. Ultimately I didn't forget my mother's adage, "No matter what happens to you in your life, I know you'll be able to handle it."

I made it Mom. You were with me all the way.

Patty Jacobs lives in Eugene, Oregon with her husband Wes. She doesn't mind swimming in the rain, and often dreams of her next trip to England.